"The essence of true romance c(*romanced! You will discover the deep deep love of Christ and y(. .* *to shower it upon those you love!"*

—Glenna Salsbury, CSP, CPAE Speaker Hall of Fame
Glenna is the 2005 Recipient of the Cavett Award
and Author of *Heavenly Treasures*

"Transforming Keys is beautifully and lovingly written by Patricia Dodsworth, and her life changing message is told with such great charm. I felt myself immersed and enthralled by the simple beauty and ageless truth of Keys, swept forward in the powerful journey of the spirit. Unconventional, radical and seemingly impossible, we are exhorted to take this 'ring holder' of keys and discover the life of which we have always dreamed, overflowing with inner peace and ultimate fulfillment. This book is a spiritual GPS for life's greatest challenge."*

—Ken Howarth*

"I found the book fascinating. Patricia weaves together scriptures, poetry, quotes, and stories with some insightful and practical advice on relationships. Her forthright manner and strong Christian faith allow her to tackle even sensitive topics which are often avoided. Transforming Keys *inspires couples to understand, listen, cherish and believe in the power of their faith and their relationship."*

—Dr. Cheryl Guest

*Ken Howarth is a consultant to the hospitality industry. Formerly he was a senior executive vice-president with Imax Ltd., and travelled worldwide with their various projects. Ken and his wife Lynn have two children, a fine son making an excellent start in business, and a most beautiful daughter waiting for them in heaven.

For Rachel

It is such a pleasure to gift you my little book. I believe it will reach your deep spirit!! I wish you a glorious Christmas & Blessings Beyond imagining

Love

TRANSFORMING
KEYS

TRANSFORMING
KEYS

HOPE FOR A LASTING MARRIAGE

PATRICIA
DODSWORTH

REDEMPTION PRESS

Redemption Press, PO Box 427, Enumclaw, WA 98022
functions only as book publisher. As such, the ultimate design, content, editorial accuracy, and views expressed or implied in this work are those of the author.

Unless otherwise indicated, all scripture quotations are taken from *The Amplified Bible, Old Testament*, © 1965 and 1987 by The Zondervan Corporation, and from *The Amplified New Testament*, © 1954, 1958, 1962, 1964, 1987 by The Lockman Foundation. Used by permission.

Scriptures quotations marked NASB are taken from the *New American Standard Bible*, © copyright The Lockman Foundation 1960, 1962, 1963, 1968, 1971, 1972, 1973, 1975, 1977, 1995. All rights reserved.

Scriptures quotations marked TM are taken from *The Message Bible* © 1993 by Eugene N. Peterson, NavPress, PO Box 35001, Colorado Springs, CO 80935, 4th printing in USA 1994. Published in association with the literary agency—Alive Comm. PO Box 49068, Colorado Springs, CO 80949. Used by permission.

Scriptures quotations marked NIV are taken from the *Holy Bible, New International Version®, NIV®*. Copyright © 1973, 1978, 1984 by Biblica, Inc.™ Used by permission of Zondervan. All rights reserved worldwide. WWW.ZONDERVAN.COM

Scriptures quotations marked NKJV are taken from the *New King James Version*. Copyright © 1979, 1980, 1982 Thomas Nelson, Inc. All rights reserved.

Scriptures quotations marked NLT are taken from the *Holy Bible, New Living Translation*, copyright © 1996, 2004 by Tyndale Charitable Trust. Used by permission of Tyndale House Publishers, Wheaton, Illinois 60189. All rights reserved.

Scripture quotations marked KJV are taken from the King James Version of the Bible.

Scripture quotations marked ASV are taken from the *American Standard Version* of the Holy Bible, first published in 1901 by Thomas Nelson and Sons.

Chapter 25 "Under the Knife" by Rona Maynard: copyright Rona Maynard, used by permission.

Chapter 7 "God Holds the Key" by Geoffrey T. Bull: copyright Moody Publishers, used by permission.

Chapter 3 "From Now On" by Ralph Shallis: copyright Gospel Folio Press, used by permission.

ISBN 13: 978-1-63232-205-0

Library of Congress Catalog Card Number: 2009904363

CONTENTS

ACKNOWLEDGMENTS

DEEP GRATITUDE TO the wonderful girls who have been part of the Transforming Keys team and have encouraged, exhorted, and prayed during the writing of this book. You know who you are, and each of you is known.

Jean, faraway in England, your phone calls, wisdom, and prayers have been such a source of strength. Thank you.

To the fine people at WinePress Publishing and, lastly, to the ever-patient and detailed editors, Cindy, Judi, and Barbara, thank you.

It is only right to acknowledge that "the gracious hand of my God was upon me" without blaming Him for the shortcomings, which are all mine!

DEDICATION

Beloved Steve,

My heart bursts with desire to dedicate this book to you. Without your unflagging encouragement it would never have been completed.

I love your passion for truth, and your great desire for these principles to wonderfully carry the readers forward in their own journeys.

As for the dance of our marriage, thank you for choosing me so long ago. Through rain and storm and sun, God has made our love a shore-less sea.

INTRODUCTION

TOTALLY DEJECTED, TWO of them decided to walk home. Their poverty did not allow a donkey. It would be seven miles and less than safe as the dusk gathered, but what was there to stay for? Three years of hope, three years of long walks and careful instruction had ended on Friday. The teacher had been executed.

As they struck out north through the city gates and beyond the crumbling walls, a stranger approached them, raising his eyebrows in question.

"Yes, you can walk with us." It was dangerous alone, and three would certainly be better than just two. They plodded on in silence for the space of half an hour.

"So why the gloom and doom?"

"When did you come to town?" one asked. "The prophet, he died on Friday. We thought he was the Promised One." The sad story all tumbled out—teacher, healer, friend, three wonderful years. There was to be hope for the downtrodden, blessing for the nation, maybe promotion for themselves.

"Now He is dead, truly dead. He is cold and buried. Another very disturbing thing, some of the girls in His following went early to the tomb this morning, and His body has been stolen."

It turned out that the stranger was a young rabbi and very knowledgeable. "When the Promised One came, wasn't He supposed to die? Did the prophets not declare He would be sacrificed and pay for sin? Did the Baptizer not announce Him as the Lamb of God?"

The journey passed so quickly. The young rabbi walked them through the whole of the Old Testament with clarity, purpose, understanding, stupendous truths, heartwarming revelation. It was dark when they reached Emmaus, scarcely a village, pushed open the wooden door, and groped for the lamp.

"Won't you stay?" The new friendship, the cushions, the warm glow of the lamp, the simple fare—there was something timeless in the moment.

Then it happened. He reached for the bread and broke it to share with them. There were red gaping scars on His hands. Looking up they saw His face. It was He—Jesus—their teacher, their friend. They both gasped in astonishment, and then He was gone.

All dangers were forgotten, and they set off the same night to go back and tell the others.

As you journey through these chapters, may your heart, like theirs, be warmed. Christ himself will travel with you by His Spirit.

CHAPTER 1

ONE UNIQUE YOU
IN ALL THE UNIVERSE

EVERY LIVING PERSON on the planet is one of God's originals, not even a limited edition. Each one of us has a biological signature—a very personal DNA. Our Designer is artistic and creative, and each of us is one of His crowning achievements.

Can you put aside your preconceptions and arguments and open your mind and heart to ask, "How can I become the man or woman God created me to be?" Will you dare to read—even study—the instructions on how to do so?

I have been married to my husband, Steve, for thirty-seven years. We have two married children and three delightful grandchildren. As a young mother and wife, I had a deep sense of my own need and personal hunger. I wanted to know what God thought about me—as a woman. I wondered where I should begin my search to find His plan for me.

One day I noticed my father looking something up in a very thick, heavy book.

"What's that?" I asked.

"It's a dictionary," he replied, "a dictionary of Greek and Hebrew words."

I asked if I could borrow it. I thought it would fit perfectly into my search for source material. I wasn't interested in a book of opinions; I was eager to find answers for myself. Thus began the most satisfying research I had ever taken on. I still have that old *Strong's Concordance* that I borrowed, now well-worn and barely intact. It was a long lend. Thanks, Dad!

On and off over the following six or seven years, I studied and researched ancient key words. What I learned from the scriptures both stunned and thrilled me. I ended up with an untidy pile of notes full of exciting discoveries.

Over the years I have taught these "Transforming Keys" around kitchen tables and to larger groups. I, and others who have studied with me, have found biblical truths from long ago that have incredible application to our contemporary lives. The women began to call these truths "Rubies," taken from the scripture in Proverbs 31:10 (ASV): "A worthy woman who can find? For her price is far above rubies."

I invite you to come with me and share my discovery. We will go back to the original languages and uncover instructive secrets that have been found to be real and meaningful today.

It's always the same. The biblical truths cause a rising in my heart along with the passion to share them. You can be certain that God can solve all issues and will meet your very deepest needs effectively, because He not only designed you but also inspired the writing of His instruction book. Sharing this discovery is a spiritual matter with its own battles. Each time I have the opportunity to share publicly, a sense of weakness comes upon me.

One evening before a night class, Steve called me from his office.

"How are you doing?"

"Not good," I told him. Between nerves, self-doubt, and battling with the devil, I was in the middle of what I came to call *personal reduction*.

Steve said, "I'm coming home to make tea for you." Tea is the English solution to every crisis—large or small. We sat together as he poured tea into my cup and truth into my mind and heart.

"Trisha," he said, "in what you are going to teach tonight, wonderful applications of scripture to contemporary lives, you are carried along by the flow of a mighty river. It is eternal and unalterable truth. You cannot fight the unstoppable current. To do so would be like standing in the middle of the Amazon, there to raise your flag and hope to stop its vast waters. You would only batter yourself to death. God wrote the original manuscript by His Holy Spirit. He hasn't changed His mind. He will not rewrite the script despite our convoluted efforts to do so. We can safely push against this fortress of truth because it will not move. What He has said and decreed about our lives on earth is fixed in heaven. He will not revise it to accommodate the changes in our culture."

"Thank you, Steve, your encouraging words under-girded and fortified me." I went into the evening un-afraid.

Please don't think that I have it all together. Nothing could be further from the truth. In a split second I can forget what I know to be true and choose my own way or an easier path. I find my tongue unkind, my words thoughtless, and I catch my heart wandering away. Oh, yes! I still blow it. I still fail. I remain a Christian who struggles. But I am on a great adventure with Jesus.

These ancient keys are for you, and they will open doors that you never dreamed possible. Christ always comes through to prove that His Word is true. The principles we will explore are so practical that you will be astonished again and again that a book so old can be so relevant, and can have such a transforming effect on our lives. Hardly a day goes by that I don't have the opportunity to put one or more of these truths into practice.

Once we know the facts, does life become a pushover? Not at all. Struggles may well increase! You will discover that you have an adversary—the devil himself. He hates these principles because they are diametrically opposed to his agenda. His design is to obscure, to manipulate, and to change the parameters of truth. His continuous deception is to mix in a little truth with diabolical lies. What you are about to unwrap is in many ways opposite to what is being fed in large doses to this bewildered generation. Alas, our best carefully laid plans for our future come adrift and disconnected from our hopes. We plot and plan our times of pleasure, spinning dreams of un-interrupted bliss, yet reality at times has a way of undoing our expectations.

So here we are. You are on the guest list that God drew up before the earth had foundations. I truly believe He planned that you would pick up this little book and explore it for yourself.

Welcome! I am excited to share these chapters with you. As you take tiny steps of obedience to God's personal call and design for women of all ages, you will experience the gentle rain of heaven watering and nurturing your life. You will draw close to Him, and He will respond. You will be amazed to find the Creator of the universe lovingly listening.

Many years ago, Steve was honored at Buckingham Palace. He and both his parents received gilt invitations under the seal of the Duke of Edinburgh. When they arrived at the palace, they were stopped at the gate by several guards so that their identity could be verified. Upon admission, all three were led into a long, magnificent picture gallery where the waiting began. Steve doesn't wait well. Red carpet, hanging crystal, and enormous gold-framed portraits of people he doesn't know are not really his forte. They waited there for more than an hour. Finally, one of the staff came, and much ado was made of the "meet and greet" procedure.

"Stand in a line. Upon your turn, inching forward, face His Royal Highness, bow, take three steps forward and shake hands, back up without turning round again, bow a second time, avoid bumping into the next in line as you reverse."

After this was practiced several times, all concerned entered the central ballroom—white, red, gold, and vast! The order of those to receive an award needed, of course, to be the same order as the announcements. This took much time and care to arrange. Other guests and family members were escorted to tiered seats. When everyone was seated, a small orchestra played for a long time. Finally, the double doors opened, the music stopped, all stood, and the ceremony began.

How very different this setting was from when Prince Charles comes back to his parents' home for an early breakfast. The guards recognize his face and his car. The Aston Martin spits gravel in the courtyard, the footman swings open the door, and the prince tosses his coat to an attendant and dashes inside. "Morning, Mum, is Dad joining us?"

This warm relationship and sense of belonging are what Christ was trying to explain with "*Our* Father in Heaven," and then the sweetest thing He ever said was, "I am ascending to *your* Father."

"Thus says the LORD, 'Stand by the ways and see and ask for the ancient paths, Where the good way is, and walk in it; and you will find rest for your souls.'"
—Jeremiah 6:16 NASB

CHAPTER 2

WHAT TIME IS IT?

"EXCUSE ME, COULD you please tell me the time?" We look at our watches, our screens, our cell phones, our Blackberries. We have raced past that question, and in the rush tumbled into the latest fad for relaxing, the miracle diet for reducing, or the best excuse for leaving our husbands.

What time is it for women on planet earth? Is it time to weep and mourn? Our Creator's plan for us has somehow been distorted. Our dignity has been degraded. Have we lost our way? Does our true destiny elude us?

Satan has ravaged our lives in subtle disguise and has given us a list of reasons to behave in ways that damage our own femininity. Someone has trampled on our innocence and stolen our virginity. Perhaps our mothers failed to share with us that our bodies were to be protected in purity rather than inflamed with lust.

Have we women been robbed of those fulfilling relationships we crave and made to believe that our identity is found in ruling and controlling others? Do we skillfully use the weapons of manipulation and rebellion? Have we dismantled the protective covering in the headship of our husbands, demoting our warrior men by our thoughts and the things we say? No one taught us that to respect them is to prompt them to protect us. Have we lost touch with the power and magnetism of a quiet spirit that should be undisturbed in us and un-disturbing to others?

We have been told that meekness is weakness and is spilled out on doormats, and so this priceless treasure has been eclipsed by our demands to be in charge. Without this precious jewel of meekness adorning both our days and nights, we have an inner sense of desolation. We can never seem to find the keys that unlock the castle of satisfaction and rich relationships, and nothing relieves our deepest thirst.

Are there solutions to these dilemmas? Is there a personal God out there? Does He really care, and will He help us? There are times when we know at the roots of who we are that God exists. He is the one Who spoke the whole universe into existence and sustains it all by just saying so. We topple over the edge into insanity when we deny the evidence of His design in the creation all around us. "Because that which is known about God is evident within them; for God made it evident to them" (Romans 1:19 NASB).

Perhaps we know about Him, but we have excluded Him, pretending He isn't there. As we have elbowed our way past the boundaries, have we ignored His laws and forgotten that we can please Him? Now we feel bewildered and lonely. As we mourn our state of affairs, we seek every conceivable panacea rather than stretch and struggle our way back home to His heart.

Are you still wondering what time it is? It is time to assess the damage and clear the rubble. It is time to rebuild the walls that protect our families, our husbands, our children, and ourselves. It is time to set a watch over our hearts and to fortify the gates into the city of who we are. If we do not have a biblical benchmark for our decisions, we will be awash in a culture that has lost its way. It is time to search for God with all of our beings. It is time to respond to the King of the universe, the Creator of all things. We need to find out who He really is and what He has in mind.

God's original dream for us is glorious. His voice, faster than the speed of light, travels to our hearts, calling us to come to Him. His design is to recover us and establish us solidly in His household as members of His own family. Because He is the King of all things, we become His royal daughters. Christ's sacrifice on a jagged hill above Jerusalem more than two thousand years ago is the gateway that will lead us home. We come home to significance and meaning, to joyful relationships, hope, and expectations. To grasp this awesome truth is to experience changes in our thinking that will soak into our very beings and transform us.

It is time to discover His call on our lives. It is time to know that nothing is impossible with Him and to learn the secrets of His design for us. There is a castle with your name on the gate. You can receive the keys forged for women in the fires of eternity, then take them and unlock the well-furnished rooms that await you. In some of these rooms we will kick off our shoes and rest our weary bodies; in others we will work hard, and it will seem to cost us our life's blood to keep them free from debris and pollution. Other rooms will awe us as we discover that they are full of unexpected treasures.

It is time to believe that the wounds Jesus Christ received to His own body were for each of us personally, and that our names are engraved on His pierced hands. It is time to wrestle the awesome truths of the New Testament into our hearts. It is time to take the words and the promises and make them personal and to discover that Christ's cross intersects with everything that challenges us in this life. This cross is more than a symbol or a Christian sign. It comes in the Holy Spirit's revelation to our hearts from the very person of Jesus himself. He reaches deeper than all of the holes we may dig for ourselves. He finds us there and rescues us.

We have His very image stamped on us. This is how we have been created. Our hearts and consciences bear witness to God's voice calling us to come. We can feel His supernatural life within and experience His power in the nitty-gritty of living. When we take hold of this, we receive from Him a poise that enables us to company equally with kings or beggars. It is time to assert that Jesus is for us not against us; He will receive and restore the most unrecoverable.

Christ is the only One Who gives safety and completeness. He alone can bring life to relationships long destroyed and dead. *It's Him! It's Him!* In our frenzied searching, all other solutions leave us pounding bloodied fists against the fortress of our frustrations.

My passionate cry is that you will take the journey. As you surrender your heart to the loving Creator God, you will find that Jesus Christ is enough for your past and your forever. He has the power to give into your hands these secrets, these Transforming Keys.

Born for Palaces

Its turrets glisten, flags fly free.
How can this castle be for me?
To find my way between those walls
That beckon me to splendid halls.

Then someplace deep inside of me,
A ringing call to "come and see."
A welcome song has reached my ears,
Its cadence melting all my fears.

I feel my heart so strangely drawn
And try to join them in their song.
Such words are all so new to me,
My raging thirst is to be free.

To climb that hill, my castle find,
To know some healing for my mind,
So filled with fantasies and fraud
That hold me captive from my God.

The mist is lifting, I can see
The wonders that are yet to be.
The Christ of God has come for me,
Put in my hand the castle key.

All glorious is the princess within her chamber; her gown is interwoven with gold. In embroidered garments she is led to the king; her virgin companions follow her—those brought to be with her. Led in with joy and gladness, they enter the palace of the king.

—Psalm 45:13–15

Do you like this exquisite description of how our heavenly Father sees us?

CHAPTER 3

HIS WORDS ARE DYNAMITE!

RALPH SHALLIS WAS a great unsung hero of the Christian faith. Educated in the best of British schools and from a diplomatic family posted to Spain, Ralph became an ardent follower of Christ. For many years he devoted his time to the villages of Saharan North Africa. He would approach a village, ask to speak to the elders, and offer to read scriptures and debate in a tea house.

He told us that he was not afraid of the people, but the dogs at the edge of each village were terrifying. His winning ways and gentle spirit gave him great acceptance, and over the years he discipled more than four hundred young men.

When Algeria received its independence, Christian people fled for their lives, mostly to France. Ralph was concerned that there was little in the way of good biblical teaching books in the French language. While writing a series on disciplined Christian living, he became severely ill with cancer. We met him in Belgium during this time. I still remember so clearly his deep, resonant voice, "My sons in the faith in France have sent up a wave of prayer for me. The Lord has assured me that I will live to finish this, the third book." Ralph did finish his book as the New Year commenced, and he died that year in the early summer.

In *From Now On*, he wrote:

From beginning to end the Bible claims to be the Word of God. He took at least 2,000 years to create it, using some 40 authors of most varied character, from a whole gamut of different backgrounds. These men had, for the most part, no possibility of knowing one another. Among them are found kings, philosophers, statesmen, poets, peasants, fishermen, nomads and priests. It is really a library of 66 books, a comprehensive literature of immense significance and spiritual wealth. Yet this book possesses an organic unity comparable to that of the human body with its almost unbelievable complexity. It is entirely controlled by a single Divine Intelligence, just as the body is coordinated and directed from the brain. For many reasons the Bible is the most remarkable book the world has ever seen, the more so as it contains no scientific error or absurdity in spite of its antiquity...In every country and in each generation it meets man on the level of his deepest need. As we read this Book we hear the voice of God, speaking into our moral consciousness. It penetrates to our utmost heart and contains the power to transform it into the image of God.

*M*an [woman] shall not live by bread alone, but by every word that proceeds from the mouth of God.

—Matthew 4:4 NKJV

Jesus clearly points out that physical food is not enough to sustain life. If we really want to do more than exist, we must feed on the words God speaks. If I were to give a single recommendation to every human being on the earth, it would be to take the written scriptures in his or her favorite version and keep it in his or her presence. Then read it and write out the parts that speak to them; search it, meditate on it, personalize it, and let it become food and drink to their spirits.

The results would be explosive. One of the most powerful, life-giving components of what we have come to call "Transforming Keys" is that it is a track for you to run on. It provides equipment for your climb. Women are shown a simple way to interact privately and personally with the living and active words of God Himself.

Martin Luther said that he studied the Bible as he gathered apples. First, he shook the whole tree that the ripest might fall. Then he shook each limb; and when he had shaken each limb, he shook each branch, and finally twigs and leaves. The implication is to search the Bible as a whole, shaking the whole tree. Read it rapidly as you would any other book. Shake every limb by studying book after book; then shake every branch, the chapters, when such divisions do not break the sense. You will even be rewarded if you look under each leaf by searching the meaning of the words because their richness will touch your spirit.

Before the triune God began to speak life-giving words to our planet, it was an empty waste without distinguishable form, and darkness was on the surface of a very great deep. Yet something was going on; someone was moving over the face of the dark waters.

What happens to the human heart when the Spirit of God begins to move and communicate? In Genesis 1:3 we read God's own words of command over the emptiness, "Let there be light." As we sit and copy the scriptures relating to God's plan and dream for us, we discover something miraculous taking place. Our dark thought patterns and attitudes begin to change and we start connecting with the one true, dynamic source of light and life.

Early in our marriage, Steve walked through the kitchen one morning and casually remarked, "I just copied out some verses from my morning reading."

I wondered if I had heard him correctly and asked, "You what?"

He repeated himself.

"Why would you do that, I mean, it's already written out for you?" Actually, at this time he did not know that the kings of Israel, once established on their thrones, were instructed to copy out by hand all of the scripture that they had in their day.

"I do that all the time," Steve continued. I was about to learn of an invaluable personal key. To copy out the inspired Word in our own handwriting was God's idea. We, too, can enjoy these kingly benefits for the price of a notebook. He (the king) shall keep it with him, and he shall read in it all the days of his life,

- That he might learn [reverently] to fear the Lord his God,
- …by keeping all the words of this law and these statutes and doing them,
- That his [mind and] heart may not be lifted up above his brethren [note the defense against personal pride]
- And that he may not turn aside from the commandment to the right hand or to the left;
- So that he may continue long, he and his sons, in his kingdom in Israel.

(See Deuteronomy 17:18–20).

In the longest psalm, Psalm 119, the writer magnifies the wonder of God's Word in every verse. God blew His own life-giving breath into the original scriptures as prophets and apostles painstakingly wrote word by word.

Sheila, who participated in the very first "Rubies" class, began to copy down scripture. She expressed, "It was as if Jesus stood right beside me as I wrote."

Dr. Ross Hastings, former senior pastor at Peace Portal Alliance in Greater Vancouver, said, "When we encounter the Word it regenerates us. You cannot encounter Jesus and not be changed."

In Hebrews 4:12 we discover that the words we copy from the Bible are living and active; they are sharper than a two-edged sword; they penetrate even to divide a soul and a spirit, joints and marrow; they judge the thoughts and attitudes of the heart. The Word of God changes us, turns us around, refreshes us, and feeds us. When we read the beginning of the gospel of John, the Word of God is declared to be Christ Himself. He has promised His Spirit to be your teacher. He will show you the way and conduct you on your journey.

As He opens the scriptures to you, you will have the same experience as the two disciples in the introduction. At their lodging in Emmaus, they were among the first to feel His resurrection power. They said to each other, "Were not our hearts burning within us while He was speaking to us on the road, explaining all the scripture to us?"

The Scriptures Cleanse Us

"You are already clean because of the word which I have spoken to you."

—John 15:3 NASB

Have you ever felt the citadel of your soul being invaded and soiled? At such times, turn to the Bible, begin to read the powerful words, and be cleansed.

The Scriptures Bring Joy to Us

Jeremiah, the prophet, was in dreadful circumstances, described as "having pain that is perpetual" and "as a wound that is incurable." He cried to God to remember him and to take notice of him, for he was sitting alone. In the middle of all of this he shares with us a timeless secret: "Your words were found, and I ate them, and Your words were to me a joy and the rejoicing of my heart" (Jeremiah 15:16). So could it be, when our joy level is low and our hearts are swamped with anxiety and fears, we should consider when we last engaged vitally in the Holy Scriptures? Let us follow Jeremiah so that we can say that we found, we ate, and God's words were a joy and caused us to rejoice.

Jesus identified Himself when He said that He was truth. So it is He, and He alone, Who comes to us in splendor and majesty. He comes to bring freedom—freedom from fear, anxiety, addictions, and destructive life habits. He has taken everything we will face in life, from beginning to end, into His own crucified body. At the cross He dealt the death blow to whatever has the power to hurt us. By drawing close and identifying with Him, we participate in His victory over that very thing that threatens to destroy us. "I have been crucified with Christ; and it is no longer I who live, but Christ lives in me" (Galatians 2:20 NASB).

This is absolute truth. Believe it and live. When we pick up our Bibles we enter a land whose borders are drenched with the blood of men and women who have died because they believed it. Many were burned at the stake for translating it into English. We don't have to search far to learn of people who risked their lives through the centuries to bring its message of hope to the farthest reaches of the earth.

We neglect the contents of God's Word at our own peril. We study it so as not to be ashamed or disfigured ourselves. We pursue its pages to find Him, the God Who is the most effective communicator in the universe. We copy out the words to extricate ourselves from habit focus if we are familiar with the text. This slows us down to give the divine Counselor, the Holy Spirit, time to speak light into our darkened minds. We are inexorably drawn to the cleansing and the freedom. There will be for you a lightness of spirit and the beauty of His new life within you. Who doesn't want to get started?

My first recollection of Mara was of an attractive woman confidently striding down a city street, hand-in-hand with her two boys. She cut a perfect picture of Canadian motherhood. Later both of us were at a party, and I wondered if we could be friends. I decided that in her corporate glory she was up there somewhere beyond reach. Time passed and Mara fell sick.

As the winter approached, we were enjoying a day on the ski slopes when someone mentioned that they had seen Mara. Although very unwell, she was, nonetheless, out on the hill. Somehow I knew I had to find her, and when I did, I was astounded. She was barely recognizable. There seemed to be little left of her as she bravely tried to ski with her family. She had lost forty pounds. Mara was anorexic. On that snow-packed hill I felt sure that God was calling to me to reach out to her.

Back in our home town, it seemed impossible to find her. Finally I reached her husband, Michael, and he told me that she was in a psychiatric ward at a facility in another city. He said that I could visit her if I wished. He had been there with her for many days, but now was needed by their children at home.

As I drove to visit her, I wondered and prayed about what to bring her and what I would say. My own journey exploring God's purposes for me had just begun. The Word of God was reaching into the roots of my being. Why not share my new discoveries with Mara? Besides, I couldn't think of anything else.

For me, there is always a certain aroma I notice in hospitals. It's not unpleasant, but it reminds me that everyone is there because he or she is unwell. The psychiatric ward was no exception. I found my new friend crunched up in bed, skeleton-like.

"Would you like to dress and go for lunch at a really cool place?" I asked.

I was surprised and delighted when she jumped at the suggestion and signed herself out. While she played with her lunch, I began to express the love of God to her. She was amazed that I didn't reject her in the condition she was in. Slowly but surely, I was able to explain to her God's design for us as women, and His personal plans of only good for her.

By the Lord's grace, and in these most unlikely circumstances, I saw hope begin to kindle in her eyes. The Bread of Life was nourishing her from the scriptures. Over time, the person of Christ, through the written scriptures, began to have a healing effect on her heart and mind and then, slowly, on her body.

Weeks later, on one of my subsequent visits, she simply packed her bags and checked herself out. She was one excited lady, turning her steps toward home, to her husband and children. She has never looked back. I tell you this story to point out the powerful simplicity of sharing biblical truth with a desolate and dying soul. Mara went on to a deeply fulfilling life. For your interest, many years later, in a period of excruciating trouble and difficulty for Steve and me, Mara and Michael stood closely beside us.

Does your heart hunger to know its purpose, its destiny? There is a castle that belongs to you. There are ancient keys to open the doors. Your major contribution is to set aside a small amount of time each day to become the man or woman God created you to be.

Has your privilege, as mine, been to fall headlong, deliriously, passionately in love with someone you eventually married? If so, how important was it for you to spend time alone with him without the presence of friends or relatives? I know the answer is that it was extremely important.

Was meeting your beloved something you forced yourself to do under obligation, or was it something you planned, arranged, and even disciplined your time to make happen?

Before we were married, Steve and I, at a busy conference in London, could not get time together. The conference grounds were alive with people we knew, and the London streets teemed with crowds and traffic. Enormous red buses ground past us, belching out black diesel fumes. It seemed impossible to find a quiet place and an undisturbed time to be together.

Nevertheless, Steve is a great conniver. Carefully following his instructions, I found him once in a graveyard behind an ancient church. There, like Wilberforce's Clarkson, we shared a carton of yogurt between the resting forms of two very tired old men. It became a daily ritual.

Imagine that the one you love let it slip that the time the two of you spent together was an obligation rather than an irrepressible desire? I have heard it implied that regular devotion to Christ in terms of time spent reading or studying His Word and in prayer indicates a certain bondage or legalism. In one respect, I must wholeheartedly agree! If there is no love relationship, no desire, then leave your Bible to collect the dust of the days and the years. The tragedy, however, is that the meaning of your life will disintegrate, and the power to enjoy it—even on the simplest level—will become elusive.

Come with me, if you will, and let us experience the magnitude and stunning effect of the night sky. Let us find a hill, a spot where we can lie on our backs without the intrusion of any light except perhaps the moon and the stars and planets themselves. Do they call to you? Do they answer to the immense vastness, the great capacity you sometimes feel inside?

They are declaring to you Christ their Creator's glory. They are calling to you, telling you of your ability to receive, by grace alone, His very person into yours. The heavens declare the glory of God. The universe is a reflection of our cosmic loneliness and interior vastness. How can this be? The heaven of heavens cannot contain Him, yet He dwells with those whose spirits are crushed to powder. God Himself gives us the capability of knowing His presence.

You might like to enjoy and ponder these two quotes and the following poem:

Blaise Paschal, brilliant French mathematician, scientist, and philosopher wrote: "There is a God-shaped vacuum in the heart of every man, put there by God Himself that can only be filled with the person of Jesus Christ."

Saint Augustine of the fifth century said, "Oh, God, Thou hast formed us for Thyself, and our hearts are restless 'till they find their rest in Thee."

Reclusive English writer Frances Thompson gave us a deep and compelling poem, 'The Hound of Heaven," disclosing our wayward hearts. God Himself is portrayed as heaven's hound, pursuing us:

I fled Him, down the nights and down the days;
I fled Him, down the arches of the years;
I fled Him, down the labyrinthine ways
Of my own mind; and in the mist of tears
I hid from Him, and under running laughter,
Up vista-ed hopes I sped....

You will be stabbed with a thrilling awe at the persistent, steadfast pursuit of the living God, Who is intent on gaining your heart and releasing to you the life you were created to live.

Let's explore and discover these keys together. Let me introduce you to the most elegant and gracious of companions. They will trip lightly out of the King's palace if you call to them and then you can walk a few miles with each one.

CHAPTER 4

OUR FIRST ROYAL
COMPANION, PRUDENCE

PRUDENCE HAS NOTHING to do with being prudish, proper, or puritan. Rather, it is a desirable attribute in a woman, giving her remarkable appeal, and is to be cultivated. "A prudent wife is from the Lord" (Proverbs 19:14 NASB).

One of God's gifts to a man is a prudent wife. What do you think she looks like?

As usual, I had been dropping hints. In my mind it had become a serious issue that required an immediate decision. In the privacy of our cold garage, and with my mind working overtime, I cornered my husband, Steve. I knew what I wanted and planned to get his agreement before he could object or express his opinion.

A wonderful family had made a road trip of more than one thousand miles to come and visit us. They had stayed longer than expected, and we were to receive relatives from overseas in just two more days. I was certain I needed time to unwind and get ready. We simply had to let our current guests know the situation.

"You must ask them to leave," I blurted out.

I will never forget his reply, "Trishie, don't do this to me."

I was smitten. Didn't I believe that God must have a timetable and it would really help if I cooperated? Slowly, I was given a change of heart. Why was I making such a fuss? I would abandon my anxiety to God's program and Steve's sense of timing. A certain quietness began to displace my agitation. I knew it was His peace.

Once I settled down, the two remaining days were full of fun and richness. Hide-and-seek with the children on a rocky point below a lighthouse, barbeque, children's stories, and deep meaningful conversation among the adults late into the evening. It was hard to let them go. When they did, I cared for linens and laundry while Steve, maybe now a little contrite, vacuumed the whole house. I was still learning about prudence.

Let's begin an exciting and simple exploration of the original languages of scripture. You will discover, as I did, that the defining elements of the words, along with some of these notes, give us the "how to behave and what to do" answers to our questions.

In Hebrew, *prudence* means to be and act circumspectly (examine carefully, be watchful), to behave oneself wisely, and be considered wise.

Prudence is not a virtue we are born with. We must train ourselves in it. As a woman, I think I see the situation clearly, and I am ready with my quick, well-packaged answer. My husband, on the other hand, is struggling through the issue and working hard to verbalize his thoughts.

If I jump in too soon I will short-circuit his all-important need to express what he thinks. Prudence teases out his thoughts, and we discover in the end that his conclusion will often encompass more than my quick answers. Not to mention how wonderful he thinks I am for listening so intently.

Don't you think we need to set the stage for more Napoleonic experiences for the man of our dreams? Napoleon conquered much of Europe! Instead of quenching your husband, try deliberately expressing your confidence in him. Listen as if he were the only one in the world who speaks your language. Concentrate on what he is saying. Give him the respect of your intelligent questions.

Periodically my husband will say something like, "Thanks so much for listening to me," and I think, *Wow, that wasn't so hard.* I actually didn't do very much at all, but it was so deeply appreciated!

Let's look at what is opposite to circumspect from our definition above: impulsive (hasty and impetuous), reckless, under the sway of one's emotions (swept away).

We so easily say, "Oh, my feelings ran away with me." Here are two reflections regarding my speech:

1. If only I had been prudent and calm, how differently the evening would have turned out.
2. I did keep quiet; I was watchful and vigilant, and look what happened!

By being prudent, I refrained from shooting off my mouth and sweeping my husband off the table before he had an opportunity to express his own thoughts. Guess what? He did have an opinion, and one worth listening to. I would have missed this if I had proceeded as usual.

The big topic of conversation on a walk along the river was whether or not to purchase a car from friends. There was nothing wrong with the car; it was a new model with a leatherette roof. Nor was there a problem with the friends. But somehow it didn't sit comfortably with me. Steve launched into detailed descriptions of the car and talked and talked. I was just beginning to try on this prudence bit, and I saw my chance. Suddenly he turned and asked, "What do you think, Trish?"

It would have been so easy, so natural, to tell him exactly what I thought, but I said, "Wow, I can see you really like that car." That was all he needed to start up again and talk about the horsepower, the leather seats, the payments, and how it might improve his business.

Then he stopped on the trail and asked again what I thought.

"I can see you really are working through the details on this one."

What happened next? You guessed it. He was still wrestling down the answer. Then for the third time he turned and asked for my opinion. I promise you I didn't give it. His response, with only the slightest hint of exasperation, was, "You're a lot of help."

Then, without losing stride, he began deliberating about the value of appearance in business. All of a sudden he stopped and said, "This is backwards." He proceeded to give his reasons for not buying the friend's car. I could hardly believe it. I had made room for him to talk out the particulars and in the end his conclusion was the same as mine. I hadn't forced anything; in fact, I had hardly said a word.

I promise you that if you cultivate intelligent and eager listening, and refuse to push your opinions, he won't make any major decisions without conferring with you.

"Oh," you say, "so you do give your opinion." Of course, but often not before I have made room for my husband to go through the all important verbalizing process himself without my trying to control or manipulate the outcome.

Let's listen. It's part of our role as women.

CHAPTER 5

OUR SECOND ROYAL COMPANION, GRACIOUSNESS

SWANTON MORLEY IS a picturesque village in the lovely countryside of Norfolk, England. Driving between the brick houses, we follow a winding road to the ancient stone church. Here we turn onto a lane, ever narrower, and follow it until we come to a small wood-faced cottage at the very far edge of the village. We are surprised by the beauty of the garden; it boasts some of the finest roses grown in England.

I ring the buzzer and soon hear an electric click in the door and step inside. The room I enter holds one of our earth's most precious people.

Although I was expected, Jean did not come to the door and does not rise to greet me. I have visited her here for ten years, and she has never risen to greet me. Jean has been paralyzed for forty-two years. When she was a young mother, pushing a buggy with her two babes in it, she lost her footing on a curb and fell. That morning was the last time she ever lifted an infant from the crib, ever cooked supper for her family, or ever walked.

Today I find her, as always, regal and radiant. I pull a chair as close to her as possible and hold her two beautiful hands, splinted and supported with leather thongs. Many times we had spoken to each other across a vast ocean and a continent in the past year. Now we would talk face to face. What a gift God has given us in this amazing woman. I'm careful to get the time change between the countries correct, but she is always there when I phone!

From her circumscribed life she reaches around the world by prayer, by phone, and by painstakingly inscribed letters. In all the years I've known Jean, there has not been so much as a trace of self-pity or resentment. Quite to the contrary, she has embraced the goodness of the Lord on a daily basis. Jean defines a gracious woman. The following poem is dedicated to her:

A Gracious Life

So tell me now, so tell me how?
He makes His jewels so?
Do fires smart, her very heart?
Like diamonds birthed below?

Do pressures and constricting paths
Transform her edges bright?
It's choices supernatural
That make her dance with Light.

I see her smile and bear with grace,
The cross that is her load.
The Christ Who spans the ages,
With her always on the road.

"A gracious woman attains honor" (Proverbs 11:16 NASB). Notice the connection between graciousness and honor. What characterized a gracious woman in the Hebrew mind? Hebrew: *Gracious*—kind, pleasant, well favored, precious.

Notice the progression in the definition. It's like a promise. A woman who is kind and pleasant will be well-favored and viewed as precious. Often, because of our strong emotions, these characteristics are an exercise in discipline and the opposite of what we feel like doing. Nonetheless, we are called to vigorous obedience and eager awareness rather than passivity and listlessness. We learn to call on the Lord to enable us to be kind to the unworthy and pleasant to those who are difficult or rude.

God begins to change our hearts. He is always present and patiently waits to hear our call—even our silent cries. Our tiniest appeal to Him releases His adequacy.

So what does this gracious woman attain? The next key word is *honor.*

Hebrew: *Honor*—splendor, glory, respect, dignity, stateliness, and magnificence.

I believe these to be the fruits of graciousness. When I read this list, I think, *This is out of my league! I can't accomplish this; it seems too high for me, too lofty.* Yet, if these instructive definitions describe what a gracious woman receives and are in accordance with God's design for me, then I had better listen up. Unfortunately, in many situations, I find myself utterly helpless to put these characteristics into action.

But here comes the good news! When Christ poured out His life's blood on the cross, He became the gateway for me to enter into a supernatural way of living. With His own wounded hand He places in my hands the transforming key of *graciousness.* He has provided for all of us, as the King's daughters, the resources needed to choose this path. Honor will come to us as we call on the Lord in our need and sense of weakness.

It was Jean's beloved husband, Les, a heroic war veteran, who lovingly grew her roses. He brought in fresh bouquets continually while they bloomed. He cared personally and tirelessly for his darling through these four decades. Les died suddenly a year ago and went into the Lord's presence in the full assurance of the Christian faith.

Just last Thursday, when I dialed up those fifteen numbers, her first question as always was, "How are you, my dear?" If I didn't push past her selfless insistence to know of my well-being, I would never know how she really was. So gracious, she is constantly putting others first, while she has every human right to have them pay attention to her many restrictions and discomforts. Jean's nobleness of mind, her view of the world, and her sweet expressions of gratitude came out as she recounted the following:

"I was in my big chair looking out the window at red blossoms cascading downward. There was a bumble bee. I watched and watched as he went from flower to flower. He was so free. There was a little bird on a tree singing his heart out. It was after a rainstorm, and the sun came out, shining on the raindrops. God's jewels were hanging there. My spirit just flew. I don't have to pay for them. It was something very, very precious."

How would we respond if the Almighty entrusted us with such a monumental tragedy? As we accept that He uses even excruciating events to transform us, soon we will hear someone say of us, "There goes a gracious lady."

CHAPTER 6

OUR THIRD ROYAL COMPANION, DISCRETION

"As a ring of gold in a swine's snout, so is a
beautiful woman who lacks discretion."
—Proverbs 11:22 NASB

DISCRETION IS THE golden accessory to the beauty of our lives. Discretion opens the door to spacious quarters in the castle of our womanly inheritance. Immediately we notice that she has a refined bearing and presence about her. She invites us to sit with her on a beautifully appointed window seat while she shares her invaluable secrets.

In this scripture the beauty of a woman is likened to something as precious and valuable as an ornament of gold. But the bearing about of that jewel is like placing it in the snout of a pig if the woman is without discretion. None of us want to be observed as a strutting pig with a ring in her nose.

The Hebrew mind perceived *discretion* as "a taste." Have you ever gone to your fridge to discover a food item you had overlooked, and you wondered whether it was still edible or not? You smell it; it smells OK. To be absolutely certain you taste it, and then you know for sure.

The nose provides the first hint, but the taste buds make a definite and final decision. Discretion is like tasting—refined and acutely sensitive.

Hebrew: *Discretion*—intelligent behavior, judgment, to think it through.

Vine's Dictionary: *Discretion*—a call to soundness of mind and self-control.

A woman of discretion makes good judgments. There are two types of judging: judging with condemnation and judging with discernment.

In Matthew 7, Jesus taught us to not criticize and condemn others, so that we would not be criticized and condemned ourselves. The prerogative of judging in the condemning sense is God's alone.

> Behold the Lord came with many thousands of His holy ones, to execute judgment upon all, and to convict all the ungodly of their ungodly deeds which they have done in an ungodly way, and all the harsh things which ungodly sinners have spoken against Him.
>
> —Jude 14, 15 NASB

In 1 Corinthians 2, we learn from St. Paul that the spiritual man or woman judges all things. The word *judge,* as used here, means to discern. We would all like to be thought of as discerning. Discernment is another of those qualities that can be acquired with only a little effort. As we seriously engage in the Word of God, it affects our world view, our attitudes, and our values. Even our ability to discern between good and evil is a consequence of this endeavor. Consider the maturity that is the end result of this stunning scripture passage.

> Anyone who lives on milk, being still an infant, is not acquainted with the teaching about righteousness. But solid food is for the mature, who by constant use have trained themselves to distinguish good from evil.
>
> —Hebrews 5:13–14

Did you ever consider the effect hot porridge, toast, and eggs have on your ability to ski? There appears to be no direct connection between a successful descent and breakfast. However, at the top of the mountain, with the wind howling in your ears and snow biting at your face, you will desperately need that breakfast to make it down the icy slopes.

So how will we negotiate the steep places in life without the sustenance our Lord recommends? We can see that we become women of discretion by regularly engaging in the Word of God.

Oxford Dictionary: *Discretion*—not speaking out at an inappropriate time.

Webster's Dictionary: *Discretion*—to discern what is correct and proper, to judge critically (not censorious or fault-finding).

A strangely delivered message was waiting for me above Lake Lugano in Italy when our children were in their late teens. We had been in Eastern Europe on summer mission teams under the leadership of Operation Mobilization. Afterwards, our family headed to the north of Italy for several days of relaxation.

Even though we were camping, I was still making a fuss over clothes and laundry, and my disapproval was focused mostly on Geoff, our strong, handsome teenage son. My motherly instructions for folding one's sleeping bag and tidying the camping area were directed primarily at him. It seemed to me that nothing was ever quite as it should be.

My habit was to put my black Rockport sandals under the tent by the flap for the night so that I could easily find them the next day. One morning at dawn, I reached for my sandals and discovered only one. *What's this about?*, I wondered, as I scanned the grass extending to the edge of a cliff. I spotted the missing sandal about twenty meters away. Hopping over to it, I could see that it had been well chewed by some nocturnal creature but was still holding together. *There go my expensive sandals!*

That's when I sensed in my heart that the Lord was clearly speaking to me: "Stop chewing on Geoff, you're being destructive."

I was cut to the heart, and I'm sure Geoff breathed a sigh of relief when I finally eased up on him. I realized that I had been majoring in the minors.

While respect, obedience, and tidiness are all part of good parenting and it is right to affirm those behaviors, we tend to pick on the ones closest to us, the ones we love the most. This chews away at the fabric of a precious relationship. The devil is a wily opponent, and he sows judgmental and critical thoughts in our heads.

Let's consider Jesus, in human relationship with Judas, as an example of discretion. Judas was a thief and a spy. Later, he became accessory to a cruel murder. Jesus knew everything about him, yet even up to the night of His own betrayal by this disciple, Christ had not disclosed the "son of perdition" to the others. They were so uninformed that they asked, "Is it I? Is it I?"

It was John the beloved, leaning on Jesus, who asked, "Lord, who is it?"

Only then did Jesus, always full of discretion Himself, tell them, "It's the one who is dipping his bread in the bowl with me."

Our third royal companion invites us to listen, observe and learn. Throughout this chapter we have enjoyed the leisure of her window seat. As we rise she passes you a key inscribed with her name. "This is for you to keep," she says, "And then there is someone I want you to meet. Her name is Virtue."

CHAPTER 7

OUR FOURTH ROYAL COMPANION, VIRTUE

HOW DOES THE word *virtue* strike you? When I first began to regard virtue with more than casual interest, I thought of it as pristine and unattainable. I was astonished and excited to explore the biblical meaning some twenty-five years ago.

She welcomes us to a strong coffee—or tea if you prefer—as we discover this word chosen long ago by the Holy Spirit in reference to us as women. I think you will be as shocked as I was. The Hebrew word *chayil* is translated "virtuous" in only three chapters in the Old Testament.

"Who can find a virtuous woman, her price is far above rubies" (Proverbs 31:10 KJV).

"A virtuous woman [is] a crown to her husband but she that maketh ashamed is as rottenness in his bones" (Proverbs 12:4 KJV).

We women have fearsome and incredible power, not by walking over our men in high heels, but by being who God created us to be. We have the power to both crown our husbands but also to inflict rottenness so that the very structure of their persons begins to crumble.

The third reference to *Chayil* comes from Boaz, a wealthy landowner from Bethlehem, who said to the beautiful young widow Ruth: "And now, my daughter, do not fear. I will do for you all that you request, for all the people of my town know that you are a virtuous woman" (Ruth 3:11 NKJV).

Ruth was a Gentile, a foreigner from the ungodly, idolatrous country of Moab. She married the son of an immigrant family. They had left the Promised Land and the Lord's blessing during hard times. The three men of the family, including her husband, died within a decade. Ruth, however, had acquired a sense of their spiritual heritage. She chose to travel with her mother-in-law and discover her late husband's origins.

At the beginning of the arduous journey, she was moved to declare to Naomi, her mother-in-law, "Your people will be my people, and your God will be my God." In spite of her non-Jewish background, *virtue* was the signature of her life, and she was destined to become the great-grandmother of King David.

It is fascinating to discover all that is implied by the word *virtue* in the Hebrew language. As you read the following definitions, ask the Holy Spirit of God to breathe application into your own personal life journey.

Hebrew: *Virtue*—to writhe in pain, to make to bring forth, to drive away, to tremble, trust, watch carefully [patiently], to be wounded, to be sorrowful, to stay, or tarry.

Virtue—"to writhe in pain" is related in the definition to the act of childbirth.

Virtue—to cause to bring forth.

Do you ever crave to go deeper—to have a real connection with those you love? We feel safe in the presence of virtue. Much of this is somewhat mysterious, yet at the same time, very tangible. I have friends—good friends—whom I have appreciated and known for years; yet I would be hesitant to open my heart pains to them. On the other hand, some whom I haven't known for very long evoke such a sense of safety and trustworthiness that I can readily bring up some item of current pain or past anguish.

From observing the defining elements of virtue, I have come to believe that these individuals have had life experiences that have qualified them to be my confidants.

Sometimes I pray for my own marriage: "Lord, give me the quality of virtue that will cause my husband to bring forth from his heart."

Men are said to be "soul shy," yet they have an irrepressible need to share their deep secrets and dreams. If you are a wife or fiancée, be jealous to be the one he opens up to. It is a danger sign if he is sharing more than casually with any woman other than his own close family members. "The purposes of a man's heart are deep waters, but a man (woman) of understanding draws them out" (Proverbs 20:5 NIV).

I also fervently believe that we who are mothers need to cultivate the gift of virtue God has given us. One of the ways to do this with our children is very simple. We can devote personal one-on-one time to each child—without an agenda. This will cause them to bring forth from their hearts. God has given us an intuitive sense about them, particularly if they are troubled or in danger.

The Lord blessed our lives with two fabulous children. Our lovely, genteel, and creative daughter, Natasha, came first. Two years later our bouncing, "let-me-at-the-world" boy, Geoff, exploded into the family.

A tradition that began when they were tiny was a special time to tuck each of them into bed. There is something about being all tucked in a cozy bed that brings things up from the depths of their precious hearts. Believe it or not, this continued until they both went off to university. Sometimes those special times were brief, sometimes longer. Occasionally, in later years, when they came home they would stretch across our bed and recount what they chose to tell about their evening.

Even now, in their thirties, feet padding down to our bedroom, they bring a late-night tray of mint tea. We prop ourselves up in bed. Natasha and her husband, Jeff, pull up two chairs and chat and share, and we almost always include prayer together.

Keep those doors ajar; keep those bridges repaired and passable. You may like to get some rest when you can, because this certainly occurs both sides of midnight. These are priceless times.

The following story illustrates something very special. Our son, Geoff, was a pre-teen. Knowing he would by now be in bed, I slipped upstairs to tuck him in. His covers under his chin, he welcomed me with one of his wide, beautiful smiles. As I knelt and prayed by his bedside, I had the urge to ask him if he was OK. "Sure, Mom," he responded, his face bright and alive.

Not wanting to push, I rose and headed for his door and turned, "Geoff, are you OK?"

"Sure, Mom, I'm OK." He smiled reassuringly. Somehow I was not reassured, but I went out through his bedroom door and all but closed it.

One last time, not holding back, I asked him, "Are you really fine, Geoff?"

He burst into tears and I returned to kneel beside his bed as all the troubles poured out. Those promptings you have relating to your children are God's gifts. Don't ignore them.

Virtue—to drive away.

Virtue protects and stands its ground against invading forces. Immediately I think of family and home. We can guard against paths of compromise and blurred standards. We should be watchful and careful of dubious types of entertainment. Television programs, movie rentals, and Internet sites should be prayerfully supervised. It is no secret that in some chat rooms children have unwittingly met predators posing as their peers.

Standing our ground as parents can be costly with our children in the short-term—and with their friends. Sleep-overs, designed to be wonderful expressions of warm friendship, have sometimes disintegrated into defiling activities.

Virtue—to tremble, trust, watch carefully, patiently.

I will never forget discovering the writings of Geoffrey T. Bull, truly a Christian statesman. He lived and served the Lord in the highlands of the Tibetan border. After a wonderful start in a missionary career, he was imprisoned by the Chinese Red Army. He found himself in solitary confinement and accused of spying. This man exemplified virtue. He waited patiently and put his whole trust in God, although "We shall be compelled to execute you tomorrow" was the specter he lived with continually. This is part of one of his powerful poems birthed in extremity and isolation.

> The day will dawn when we will say, "Do you remember?
> The fiery trial passed away, a dying ember?
> And from the furnace in burnished gold, skilled hands will bring
> A vessel in a royal mold, to serve the King."

Somehow his spirit rose above the cramped cell and the strong iron bars of his captivity. He was released into Hong Kong with only a shirt and pants after more than three excruciating years, but he went on to a life of fruitful service for Christ.

Virtue—to be wounded.

We are sure to be wounded in one way or another in the process of becoming virtuous. Before we look at our own wounds, let us look to Jesus as He is described by the prophet Isaiah. He was pierced, crushed, punished, and wounded.

> But He was wounded for our transgressions, He was bruised for our guilt and iniquities; the chastisement needful to obtain peace and well-being for us was upon Him, and with the stripes that wounded Him we are healed and made whole.
>
> —Isaiah 53:5

From His wounds healing virtue flows freely to us. The dysfunctional areas, those damaged places in our lives, are often the very material God uses to produce within us the most exquisite and endearing qualities.

We shared coffees, but then we needed to be alone and private. As we sat at the end of the jetty surrounded by bobbing sailboats at anchor, a beautiful, well-put-together wife and mother poured out her broken heart. Her husband had cheated on her and had come and confessed his wild fling. She truly believed his remorse was genuine. Now he wanted to rebuild their broken bridge of trust. Traveling this distance with the Lord and with her handsome husband presented her with one of life's enormous challenges. The anger, the agony, the stunned amazement, the rushing in of massive insecurities about herself—all of these were overwhelming.

We spoke about the journey of forgiveness and the grace of Christ that was available to her. We prayed and prayed some more as the weeks passed. This precious heart trusted her God against all the bruising odds and watched patiently for His hand in the restoration of her marriage. The relationship, stronger now than ever before, secures their future together and protects their children. She stands regally among those who embrace virtue in this way.

Virtue, then, is an integral part of our womanhood. It is not remote and unattainable. Many of you are more virtuous than you have ever dared to dream. Remember, when people pour out their hearts to you and feel safe in your presence, it's because God has used your own wounding to reach deeply to theirs. Perhaps this unusual sequence will give you courage as you bear your own trials.

Virtue's Path

There she stood so straight, so true,
Her eyes met mine, at once I knew
With me she wished now to converse,
Her fearsome journey to rehearse,
Of secrets from both far and wide,
She drew me kindly to her side.

At closer range I clearly saw
The ragged scars across her brow,
And though her stance was nobly meek
I saw a tearstain on her cheek.
I trembled some and wondered why
I almost felt myself to cry.

Comforted and strangely so
I chose to listen and to know
That twisted roads could be made straight
That powers of love can turn from hate
To love again, with patience wait
Till hope swings wide the longed-for gate.

She led me to a far off hill
Where crosses three stood stark and still.
I saw such anguish all for me,
The Christ of God died on that tree
To bring me back where I belong,
To make me noble, straight, and strong.

He called me then, the voice divine,
Eternity was merged with time.
My past, my present, future too

Transforming all the old to new.
'Twas then I felt my wounds so sore
My blood was spilling on the floor.

Now all those pains so well concealed
Before His searching eyes revealed.
I saw them there inside His pain,
I'll never be the same again.

So Virtue stood aside, alone,
To watch my anguished soul reborn.
To see the places of my pain
Now found in Christ to rise again,
That through my wounds His virtue flows
How can this be? His mercy knows.

CHAPTER 8

SO, WHO DO YOU
HANG OUT WITH?

"Do not participate in the unfruitful deeds of darkness,
but instead even expose them; for it is disgraceful even to
speak of the things which are done by them in secret."
—Ephesians 5:11–12 NASB

GREEK: *PARTICIPATE*—(FELLOWSHIP), TO share in company with, denoting union with, by association companionship, resemblance.

Never underestimate the influence of close friendships. Our choice of relationships in our teens and early twenties can establish a pathway for the rest of our lives. Why was my dad so concerned about me relating to a particular close friend? Our families were different, but she and I were so alike and had so much fun together. We never did anything drastic. I remember one night in our junior high years when both of us snuck out of our homes after bedtime to skate on an outdoor rink. A neighbor lady saw my dark form climbing out of a basement window and promptly reported it to my parents. It seemed such a big deal to them at the time. Granted, my darling friend enjoyed a lot more freedom than I did, and I must admit that there was a strong influence pulling me away to slippery paths.

While in grade nine I chose the gang I would run with in high school. In grade ten, when I was fifteen years old, I was flattered by the attentions of a dashing young man of twenty. While enjoying a party at a girlfriend's house, I found myself necking with this handsome hulk on her bed. Thank God, I can say necking because we never went beyond that. Shortly after, he joined the Air Force and I wore his big ring on a silver chain around my neck.

When he returned from eastern Canada I was thrilled, and having just turned sixteen, I bought a pretty sundress to celebrate his homecoming. Off we went to a party, along with the gang I had chosen for friends. It was obvious that he thought the pretty dress would look best if we were to hang it on the branch of a nearby tree. I remember us being outside and him moving his hand to my breasts. I firmly pulled away. I somehow knew it was wrong and it would quickly move to other things. Does it surprise you? That was it. I never heard from him again. My mother's prayers were being answered.

As for my girlhood friend, her paths and choices took her into dark and murderous canyons, although at times with a high-flying profile. Years later we reconnected, and the love of Jesus Christ rescued her from the powers of darkness and from her hellish lifestyle. I had three other very close friends during those years. One of them became a missionary; and tragically, one of them committed suicide. The third one I cannot trace.

Along the way, I was kicked out of high school—basically for not showing up. Too many days skipping school and hanging out at my friends' houses. We were not radical; we listened to music and danced a lot. Some days we rode the bus. Just small town stuff. My parents then tried to get me into a Christian school. When they refused to admit me, I was brokenhearted. Eventually I was accepted at a different school, although I was still wayward.

It was another three years before God's grace overtook me and completely turned my life around. During my seventeenth and eighteenth years, I was wild and rebellious in my heart. Nonetheless, I was sometimes gripped with inner conviction of my sins and gave serious thought to eternity. I knew that I was ill prepared for Christ's promised return or for death itself.

During this time I met an outgoing young man at a base-ball game. He was from Canadian Bible College in Regina and spoke very directly into my life. He strongly encouraged me to apply to the college that fall. I did just that, and what a surprise when they accepted me!

I was quickly swept into a whirl of preparation. Bedding, curtains, a teddy bear called Raunchy—all came with me to begin mandatory freshman dorm life. Putting my best foot forward, I smiled a lot and hated every minute. Soon Spiritual Emphasis week rolled around, and my heart was deeply stirred one evening when the gifted speaker instructed us from the Book of Romans. His message was all about surrendering our bodies to God as living sacrifices. I knew I had never done that, and suddenly I really wanted to. I walked forward to that simple altar in the college chapel, and the Holy Spirit gathered me up into the family of God.

So much happened in the following weeks. I remembered I had stolen lipstick from a cosmetic counter, and I wrote to the store to confess and apologize. My trusty little Bible—which I had read only to please my parents—suddenly came alive to me personally. For the first time, it made sense and thrilled me inwardly. I shall never forget kneeling in prayer with a friend in an unused music room. I felt a warm and reassuring presence, and I knew that it was Jesus.

As for the student bit, up until then I had only crammed for exams, greasing myself to slip under the door with a squeaky pass. Suddenly I really wanted to learn. What a shock to make the Dean's list and receive a scholarship that year. Jesus was changing me. That was the only time I ever received a letter from my Dad. He couldn't contain his own surprise and pleasure. God was being merciful to me, and a great paradigm shift was happening. I was now on the path of life with Him.

The years that followed were mysterious and unusual. What people thought was my marriage after graduation to a gracious man was never physically consummated. Many would not believe it, but we lived as sister and brother for nine long years. Amazingly, we were only alone for about two months during that whole time. In the Lord's goodness we were either in a college community, travelling, or had other people living with us throughout. The arrangement was legally annulled by the provincial government, and when I later married Steve I was still a virgin.

My journey has been loaded with so much privilege and adventure, along with the necessary counterpoints of periodic anguish and suffering. All of this has woven into a tapestry I would not trade for anything.

The scriptures give both guidelines and warnings about our companions, including, "Enter not into the paths of the wicked; do not go in the way of evil men" (Proverbs 4:14).

The words "Do Not Enter" are usually a warning. Don't let that be an attraction to your heart; the peril is often real, and the results can be devastating.

Proverbs 2 teaches us that when wisdom enters our hearts, knowledge becomes pleasant to our souls. We will find that both discretion and understanding will watch over us to deliver us from evil ways and from people who speak perversity.

Oxford Dictionary: *Perverse*—wayward, persistent in error.

"He who walks with wise men will be wise, but the companion of fools will suffer harm" (Proverbs 13:20 NASB).

"A prudent woman sees the evil, but the simple pass on and are punished [with suffering]" (Proverbs 22:3).

We cannot be naïve and think that friendships are casual. Does your best friend inspire you to a closer walk with God and an uncompromising life? Breaking ties with those with whom you have had long-term relationships that have led you astray is wrenching, yet your whole future may depend on these choices.

"Do not be deceived and misled! Evil companionships [communion, associations] corrupt and deprave good manners and morals and character" (1 Corinthians 15:13).

Greek: *Corrupt*—to pine or waste, to shrivel, to wither, especially by moral influence, to deprave.

Her name was Abigail. We had enjoyed rich fellowship with her many times. She was suddenly attracted to a very clever young brain surgeon who did not share her Christian faith. She came to our tiny trailer home in Aberdeen, Scotland, for advice. There have been times in over thirty-seven years of marriage that I have heard Steve speak profoundly and with courage into someone's life. "The Lord leaves you free to choose, but you won't have His blessing if you defy Him."

Abigail seemed to really hear him, yet the next time we met she had chosen her path. She had strong and plausible reasons. We continued, of course, to be her friends, but with mounting concern. Later, when she endeavored to draw back from this unhallowed relationship, the young man went through a period of serious illness. He was quite manipulative. "Surely as a Christian you're not going to abandon me at this point," he said.

Marriage was soon on the horizon, and we were invited to visit them as a married couple in their country home. I could hardly wait to speak with Abigail alone, heart-to-heart, as women love to do. It wasn't long before we had our opportunity. The boys took off to do their "man" thing while Abigail and I went to the forest to gather treasures.

At last we could talk. Yet I could not speak my heart questions. It was as if I was gagged. There could be no meeting of minds, but much more severe was the deep sadness that there was nothing to appeal to spiritually. She was gone, and although I walked beside her, she was like some wandering star. I could neither trace nor find her. Simple obedience to the following three short verses would have saved her from much of the raw sorrow of the coming years.

Do not be unequally yoked with unbelievers [don't make mismatched alliances with them or come under a different yoke with them, inconsistent with your faith]. For what partnership have right living and right standing with God with iniquity and lawlessness? Or how can light have fellowship with darkness? What harmony can there be between Christ and Belial [the devil]? Or what has a believer in common with an unbeliever …? So, come out from among [unbelievers] and separate [sever] yourselves from them, says the Lord, and touch not [any] unclean thing. Then I will receive you and treat you with favor.
—2 Corinthians 6:14–17

Our friends and the friends of our children have a huge impact on our lives. Our choices and theirs are of grave importance in this area. We cannot take lightly the influential power of peer pressure. Pray deeply and fervently about who will enter the close circle of significant friendship in your family and in your own life.

While our hearts are always open to needy and broken people within church circles and in the wide world outside, I think that in this situation her disobedience had put out the Spirit's fire, and there was nothing to appeal to. (See 1 Thessalonians 5:19.)

CHAPTER 9

ROOM FOR ONE MORE

"We are all parts of one body and members of one another."
—Ephesians 4:25

Left Out

There we were, standing together in a closely knit circle,
Laughing, complimenting, even interrupting each other.
At one time it seemed we were all talking at once!
How comfortable we were, how easy it was to be together again.
  Why, we hadn't seen each other for a whole week.
Then, through a break in the circle I saw her,
Standing all alone, distinctly uneasy, maybe even embarrassed.
She was shifting her weight from one high heel to the other,
Now she was fumbling in her handbag.
The circle's conversation was heating up to something really
    fun, and important.
Anticipation was mounting.

In my momentary distraction I almost missed seeing her
Step out of the church door, alone.

From childhood to maturity, the matter of friendship is complex and often marked by heartbreak. It seems good at this point to put a very special key on our key ring. The key of friendship will unlock a whole new corridor of rooms to us. Some of these are well-furnished and extremely comfortable, easily entered and relaxed in, even after long periods of absence. Other rooms will welcome more furniture as the friendship grows, and some need more time! As we grow in Christ, He enlarges our spiritual capacity. We embrace an ever-increasing circle of friends, and this should leave no spaces for jealousy or insecurity. It was my dear Steve who taught me that every newcomer in any group or church is an addition, not a competition.

> One day last week a troubled heart told me of a fault which perhaps some of you have, "How can I love many people? I can love some very much, but there is not room in my heart for many." I spoke to her of the bees and how cell after cell is added to the comb and each is filled with sweet honey. Each cell is so shaped that the greatest possible number can be fitted into the smallest possible space. God, who taught the bees to do this, can do something as wonderful for us. He can add a new cell to our heart as each new person [child or grown-up] comes to be loved, and He can fill the cell full of the sweet honey of His love.
>
> —Amy Carmichael: *Edges of His Ways*

In 1 Corinthians 12 there is a long discussion on the various gifts God gives to His children. Inherent in this chapter is the undeniable truth that we, as one body in Christ, are each members of one another. This by no means diminishes our unique individuality but rather strengthens who we are together. This is what Jesus had in mind when He prayed, "That they may all be one; even as You, Father, {are} in Me and I in You, that they also may be in Us, so that the world may believe that You sent Me" (John 17:21–23 NASB).

Experience has also shown me that division in Christ's body is like tearing flesh from flesh—excruciatingly painful. In observing the unkind cutting off of certain friends from certain circles, I imagine an arm severed from the rest of the body, all alone on the coffee table. "How gross!" you say. "How inappropriate!" Exactly!

Yet sadly, this is how we can so easily act out our selfish attitudes. In Ephesians 5 the scriptures point to the amazing truth that when we belong to Christ we become part of a body with many members, each part of the other. This cuts through our independent "I don't need anybody" mind-set. Now we are part of a family—His family—and we work hard at loving and including each other.

In considering the concept of friendship rooms, my mind goes back to our beloved minister in Aberdeen, Scotland, Rev. William Still. After the Sunday evening service he would place two chairs on the lower platform below his pulpit. There he sat beside an empty chair and waited for anyone among us—out of several hundred—to come and share personal time with him. The line of people who came was an appropriate distance from the two chairs, and each patiently waited his or her turn to be with this man who so beautifully represented Jesus to us. I, too, have stood, waiting in that line of sometimes ten or twelve people, and when my time came I felt I was the only one in the whole world who mattered to him.

There is room for me in Christ's heart, so much room. He makes me feel that if I were the only lost and rebellious person in the universe, He would have come to die for me—to bring me back to where I belong.

CHAPTER 10

DON'T CHASE THAT MAN

"I adjure you, daughters of Jerusalem, by the
gazelles and by the hinds of the field, that you
stir not up nor awaken love until it pleases."
—Song of Songs 3:5

OUR LOVELY BLONDE daughter was eagerly off to Trinity
Western University in Vancouver, British Columbia, for her
freshman year. During her first week on campus, while enjoying a phone
call with her, I jokingly asked if anyone had caught her eye. She giggled
and confided, "Yes, Mum, but he's a senior and way up there. He leads
worship and plays bass guitar." She shared that she thought he looked
like a Roman centurion.

Natasha had a glorious time forging life friendships in the girls'
dorm. As for Jeff, he had certainly captured her imagination. She knew
where he studied in the library, and when she drifted by, the two of them
engaged in great spiritual conversations. Jeff was impressed with Tasha's
knowledge and understanding of the Bible. As the first term progressed,
she felt her heart increasingly drawn to him, and her feet too!

Just before her return home for Christmas break, I was researching Song of Songs, chapter three. In my trusty old concordance of Hebrew words, I discovered that to "stir not up nor awaken love until it pleases" was connected with a vow, vowed seven times over. I shared this with Natasha, along with Elisabeth Elliot's insight that God designed men to pursue, and women to respond. Elisabeth Elliot is a favorite author, and I just love two of her books, *Quest for Love* and *Passion and Purity.* In *Quest for Love* she writes, "We really don't want to do the hunting. We want you (the men) to do it."

When the spring term commenced, Natasha was determined to not pursue Jeff in any way. The amazing outcome was that he missed seeing her, and her noticed absence stirred and drew him. Yes, he pursued her, wooed her, and they became engaged and one glorious July day the next year they were wed. This summer they will joyfully celebrate ten years of marriage.

I have no doubt that Elisabeth Elliot is profoundly right. Our generation seems to have reversed the order of pursuit and response to such a degree that the winsome attractiveness of poise and gentle reserve has been substantially lost. We have replaced it by hot pursuit with hints of conniving to get what we want. Our culture gives us full permission to lower the bar as to our standard of purity. Casting aside dignity, we carelessly use our bodies to attract and catch. When the thrill of conquest is over, we are sometimes not so sure that this is whom we wanted after all. Deep inside, we girls want to be pursued, we need to be conquered.

Nonetheless, to sit still and wait, as Naomi instructed Ruth, seems intolerably difficult. Ruth of Bible times, whom we met briefly in chapter seven, has a compelling story.

She was a childless widow and a Moabite who, having left her own country and family, refused to turn back from following her mother-in-law, Naomi, to Bethlehem. It was the time of the barley harvest. Ruth, under the overruling hand of God, went out to be a gleaner. This meant that after the harvesters had passed she could gather for herself whatever was left at the corners of the field.

Without any knowledge of the local fields, she happened to stop at the part of the field belonging to a rich landowner, Boaz. Later she learned that Boaz was a distant relative of her deceased husband. As Boaz was coming out to his fields to bless the reapers, he immediately noticed Ruth and asked about her. (Remember, God is well able to alert your future life mate to your presence when He providentially draws you near to one another.) Boaz is the first to open conversation.

"Then Boaz said to Ruth, 'Listen, my daughter, do not go to glean in another field or leave this one, but stay here close by my maidens'" (Ruth 2:8).

This young woman's spirit and demeanor evoked in Boaz exactly what she was in need of—protection and direction. She didn't deliberately put herself in his way. She found she was in proximity and comported herself in an undeniably appealing manner.

You may want to stop here and read through the book of Ruth. It is only four short chapters and would not take more than twenty minutes. Pray first and ask God to make it a living story to your own spirit. Open your heart and allow Him to instruct and comfort you. May you have a deep sense of His intimate presence and care as you read. May excitement and hope rise in your heart.

As we proceed through Ruth chapter two, we discover that Boaz has already assumed the role of a generous protector. He has charged the young men not to molest her. She is invited to go to the water jugs prepared for the reapers and drink when she becomes thirsty.

Ruth speaks for the first time in verse ten in the form of a question. "Why have I found favor in your eyes, that you should notice me, when I am a foreigner?" The following verses are staggering and I can't resist including them.

Ruth is a lonely stranger. She is a destitute immigrant. She is the subject of gossip and curiosity among the wagging tongues in the town of Bethlehem. Essentially, she is a gleaner-beggar, and now she is given favor in the eyes of a wealthy and generous man.

Watch as Almighty God goes to work on her behalf. Notice that there is no striving or plotting. Instead, there is a certain gratitude springing from her heart along with the constraint of humility as she follows the advice of both her mother-in-law and Boaz.

> And Boaz said to her, I have been made fully aware of all you have done for your mother-in-law since the death of your husband; and how you have left your father and mother, and the land of your birth and have come to a people unknown to you before.
>
> —Ruth 2:11

God has provided for Ruth a man who is both aware of her and sensitive to who she is. He is able to reach and speak to her heart. Tell me, why would you settle for anything less in your prayers for a husband?

In verse twelve of this account, Boaz speaks a blessing on her: "The Lord recompense you for what you have done, and a full reward be given you by the Lord, the God of Israel, under Whose wings you have come to take refuge!"

Ruth responds with, "Let me find favor in your sight, my lord. For you have comforted me and have spoken to the heart of your maidservant, though I am not as one of your maidservants."

Now we come to one of many culminating points in this delightful account.

In verse sixteen Boaz instructs his young men regarding Ruth: "And let fall some handfuls for her on purpose, and let them lie there for her to glean, and do not rebuke her. So she gleaned in the field until evening. Then she beat out what she had gleaned. It was about an ephah of barley." (An ephah is about five gallons dry measure.)

The drama of Ruth's life is heightening. She must wait until Boaz has fulfilled all that was legally required to be a redeeming kinsman. Her mother-in-law, Naomi, wisely said, "Sit still my daughter, until you learn how the matter turns out; for the man will not rest until he finishes the matter today" *(Ruth 3:18).*

How many times the above verse has both harnessed and settled me to wait for the unfolding of God's will and purpose in my life. This is a book I have read so many times before, and yet, again today, it both thrills and excites me. Enjoy it with anticipation!

What a destiny awaited Ruth. She became part of a royal lineage that would stretch with honor to Christ Himself and on into eternity.

Characteristics to Look for in a Future Husband

- He is not merely religious but knows and loves Christ personally.
- He has a genuine love for the Word of God. (See 2 Timothy 2:15.)
- He prays easily with you.
- He is open to accountability.
- He is respectful and obedient to parents and authority.
- He is responsible, diligent, avoids debts, and is developing to his potential.
- He is sensitive to the needs of others and reaching out to meet those needs.
- He is not wanton—irresponsible, unrestrained, wild, does not dispute everything, does not disregard accepted rules.
- He is not flirtatious—playing the field for conquests.
- He is not unchaste—loose or lustful.
- He shows appreciation for the dignity of your femininity. Watch how he treats his mother.

You are looking for a mate rather than a date. This will cause you to be much more particular.

CHAPTER 11

STUNNING REBEKAH

"She girds herself with strength [spiritual, mental,
and physical fitness for her God-given task]
and makes her arms strong and firm."
—Proverbs 31:17

THE SUCCULENT MEAL of herb-roasted lamb, garlic, and leeks, with fresh baked bread, was over. Only a few dates and figs lay scattered on the polished silver tray. Darkness was falling, and the desert wind had picked up as evening drew on. A luxurious and expansive tent, well-staked, stood securely against the gusts. Expensive tapestries and well-tanned skins still held the heat of the day. Oil lamps, selectively hung from the roof cords, swayed gently, casting cozy shadows on the cushions.

Abraham was pensive, deep in thought, as he observed his strong and handsome son Isaac. The younger man reclined and watched the flicker of the lamps above his head. They were comfortable together in the silence; mutual grieving bound them, as well as their ties of blood. It was time, perhaps past time, for this son, long-promised by God to Abraham and Sarah, to have a bride. Abraham's beloved and beautiful wife of so many years now lay buried beneath a spreading oak at Machpelah. Of one thing he was certain, this maiden that would wed his son must not come from his current surroundings among the Canaanites, but from the land of his own birth.

There was strong confidence filling his heart as he instructed the steward of his household under oath. Eliezer was to go to Abraham's home country, some five hundred miles away, and bring back a wife for his son. Abraham's trusted servant took ten of his master's camels, loaded them with provisions and gifts, and made the long journey to Nahor.

It was evening, the cool of the day, many days later, when Eliezer arrived at the well outside the city. The local women came to draw water for their families. As his camels knelt down, Eliezer offered prayer:

Behold, I stand by the well of water; and it shall come to pass that when the virgin comes out to draw water, and I say to her, Please give me a little water from your pitcher to drink, and she says to me, Drink, and I will draw for your camels also, let her be the woman whom the LORD has appointed for my master's son.

But before I had finished speaking in my heart there was Rebekah, coming out with her pitcher on her shoulder: and she went down to the well and drew water. And I said to her, "Please let me drink."

And she made haste and let her pitcher down from her shoulder, and said, "Drink, and I will give your camels a drink also." So I drank, and she gave the camels a drink also.

Then I asked her, and said, "Whose daughter are you?" And she said, "The daughter of Bethuel, Nahor's son, whom Milcah bore to him." So I put the nose ring on her nose and the bracelets on her wrists.

And I bowed my head and worshiped the LORD, and blessed the LORD God of my master Abraham, who had led me in the way of truth to take the daughter of my master's brother for his son.

—Genesis 24:43–48 NKJV

Little did Rebekah know that in the preceding months she had been preparing for this hour, this point of destiny. In scripture she is described as very beautiful to look at and a virgin. Now there was nothing glamorous about giving a travel-worn stranger a drink—let alone his perspiring camels with their sagging humps and enormous capacity for water. This was far from a legitimate call on her time and energy. There was nothing exotic about the setting at all.

We observe her immediate and, I believe, spontaneous response. She quickly lowered the jar from her shoulder, saying, "Drink, and I will water your camels also." Camels can drink gallons and gallons of water. This water all had to be drawn up by hand from the well. Surely Rebekah had been accustomed to overextending herself, doing more than was expected. Notice she received an immediate reward for her efforts, a gold nose ring weighing half a shekel along with two bracelets weighing ten shekels.

This may help us as mothers not to make a big deal out of the non-critical. When your daughter comes home with a nose ring, rather than hitting the roof, say, "Honey, I love that nose ring. Do you know it's biblical?" At such moments, mother has lost nothing except the confrontation, and daughter is expected to light up, thrilled and relieved that she got the nose ring past her Mom!

It all began in a very ordinary way—a familiar place and time, a simple gesture of kindness—but Rebekah's choice was critical to her destiny. When the test comes, and it will, the strength of character built over the weeks, months, and years puts muscle into the highest choices.

This was no simple matchmaking in Genesis; Rebekah also would be part of the lineage of Christ. Soon she would be eagerly on her way to marry a man she had never seen. The hallmark of divine authenticity was on the sequence of her life events, and they all knew it. Read all of Genesis 24 for the unraveling of the whole romance.

Our days are never casual—in each one we are preparing for tomorrow.

Years ago we were honored to make the acquaintance of Dr. David Short. He was a wonderful Christian doctor and surgeon to the Queen in Scotland. While in the foxholes in World War II, he studied and learned New Testament Greek by the light of a battery-powered lamp.

My strongest memory of this generous man and his wife was their open home. They provided a bountiful drop-in Sunday lunch for university students week after week. It was my darling Steve who drifted into their large kitchen to find sinks piled with dishes and pots. Many Sundays thereafter, he rolled up his shirt sleeves to do his part and ease the load for this hospitable couple who poured out their lives for Christ and others in gentle, gracious ways.

In Rebekah's wildest dreams she never imagined that her whole future would pivot on the simple event of drawing water for ten camels and a stranger. We must remember that the most elementary of tasks can hold dignity and meaning. Nothing is trivial in the sovereign succession of life's events. Jesus attaches significance and reward to the simplest of gestures: "And whoever in the name of a disciple gives to one of these little ones even a cup of cold water to drink; truly I say to you, he shall not lose his reward" (Matthew 10:42).

As to whom we marry? This is of the greatest importance to God our Father. While we were both in Aberdeen, Rev. William Still, whose cathedral-type church was regularly filled by students on Sunday evenings, said, "There are two things that God is more concerned about than you are: whom you marry, and what you do for a vocation." Can we trust the Good Shepherd, Who is truly God and Who expressed His love in the sacrifice of His life, to lead us superbly in both of these momentous issues?

CHAPTER 12

SCORCHING WARNINGS

WHY DOES GOD seem so fussy about sex, and why is our sex drive so strong? God Himself is essentially creative. By giving us the gift of sex, He has given us the ability to not only enjoy physical intimacy but also to create eternal people. There is no relationship on earth as intimate as a vigorous marriage.

He so wanted us to enjoy highest fulfillment that He established strict moral boundaries. Keeping to these boundaries allows us to wonderfully avoid unwanted pregnancies, sexually transmitted diseases, and all sorts of guilt and depression. The biblical standard of chastity is for both security and joy. The Oxford Dictionary defines *chastity* as "abstaining from immoral or unlawful sexual intercourse."

Simply put, having sex outside of marriage is against God's moral law. It is not simply the sharing of bodies, but the intertwining of two persons, and represents a deep expression of love and togetherness within the safety of a covenant commitment. The Book of Proverbs, especially chapters 5, 7, 9, and 31, gives frank instruction about sexual behavior. The chapters are actually addressed to sons, but because they were inspired by the Holy Spirit, we as girls can gain much insight from them.

"Do not give your strength to women, or your ways to that which destroys kings" (Proverbs 31:3 NASB).

It was a surprise to discover that Proverbs 31, the searching passage regarding the priceless lady, was not written directly to women. It is an oracle to a young prince called Lemuel, and he was taught by his mother. This kind of teaching is intense—so much so that in the Hebrew mind, her words were like the piercings of a sword. They were designed to penetrate deeply into Lemuel's consciousness. They would instruct him as to whom he should avoid and what to look for in a wife. He is not to give his strength—that is, his virtue, his valor, his goods, or his might—to a loose woman.

In Elisabeth Elliot's book, *Quest for Love,* she recalls giving a speech on sexual restraint to a crowd of skeptical college students in Kansas City. They wondered, *What could this elderly lady have to say that would be of consequence to us?* They followed her message on passion and purity with rapt attention. They knew lots about passion and seemingly nothing about purity! Had they ever considered that keeping themselves pure was the supreme gift they would be able to make to a life mate? During her presentation they were riveted, and when she finished, they rose to stamp and yell their approval.

What kind of woman was Prince Lemuel instructed to avoid, and how can we learn for ourselves and teach our children to identify her characteristics? In Proverbs 5 we have the passionate appeal of a father to his son. The father instructs the son to avoid the very scenes of temptation or else he will end up giving his honor away and his future to the unmerciful. According to Hebrew thinking, he would be losing his grandeur, his appearance, his beauty, his excellence, and his glory. This path of sin will age him prematurely. The light and fire of freedom will go from his eyes. His countenance will harden.

The Holy Spirit, in His inspiration, often uses contrast. Scripture instructs us about two women in the book of Proverbs. Both women made their own appearance and the dressing up of their bedrooms top priorities. The first woman you meet is a seductress. She was engaged in promiscuous sex. She made enormous effort for the wrong reasons. "I have spread my couch with rugs and cushions of tapestry, with striped sheets of fine linen of Egypt. I have perfumed my bed with myrrh, aloes, and cinnamon. Come let us take our fill of love until morning" (Proverbs 7:16–17).

The results are damning and deadly! "'Let all who are simple (easily lead astray, wavering—Amplified) come in here,' she says to those who lack judgment. 'Stolen water is sweet; food eaten in secret is delicious!' But little do they know that the dead are there, that her guests are in the depths of the grave" (Proverbs 9:16–18 NIV).

A loose and adulterous woman is identified as "estranged and separating herself from normal habits and training." She is profane, which means that she acts with contempt toward what is sacred, including marriage. She will carelessly wound and alienate other relationships. Remember that the level of her enticement at the beginning is always exceeded by the bitterness at the end! Because the initial appeal—the attraction of forbidden fruit—is so strong, the young men who fall for her often lose interest in healthy family life and friendships. The price in hurt parents, damaged children, ruined finances, and sometimes sexually transmitted diseases is realistically not balanced by the temporary lustful excitement.

There is, of course, always a way back via the cross of Christ and His cleansing blood. Sometimes it is very difficult to re-establish the connection with God because of our inability to forgive ourselves.

Flattery: The immoral man or woman employs flattery, over-praising, and gratifying vanity to gain personal advantage.

"[Discretion shall watch over you, understanding shall keep you] to deliver you from the alien woman, from the outsider with her flattering words" (Proverbs 2:16).

"For the lips of a loose woman drop honey as a honeycomb, and her mouth is smoother than oil; but in the end she is as bitter as wormwood, sharp as a two-edged and devouring sword" (Proverbs 5:3–4).

I heard Chuck Swindoll comment aptly on this verse over the radio. He said, "Like honey-enticing persuasion, her words can pierce and kill, her words are appealing."

Here's how I would paraphrase another Proverbs passage that describes a woman like this: "I looked out of my window, though I was not observed because I was looking through the lattice. What I saw gripped, even paralyzed, my heart. It was a young man who proved to be both naïve and lacking sense. He was making a deliberate choice to walk through the street and on to the corner where he would most certainly find a wayward and immoral girl. The full bloom of day had passed, it was after twilight, and the cloak of darkness was wrapping up the evening.

Then I spotted her, seductively dressed to entice. She was deceitful and of a calculating heart. I had seen her before. She was wild and animated, undisciplined and without inhibition. She could not be found at home; she moved from the streets to the squares and loitered at every corner. Suddenly, as he approached, she grabbed hold of him and kissed him. She then launched into spiritual language outlining her religious duties of vows and peace offerings. She attempted to give some sort of religious sanction to her immoral intentions. Her voice was full of eagerness toward him. She had earnestly come to seek him out and to find him. She began to describe her sumptuous couch, so carefully prepared for both of them. She promised coverings of colored Egyptian linen sprinkled with fragrances of myrrh, aloes, and cinnamon. She cunningly set the stage, artfully appealing to both his senses and his imagination. She boldly invited him to come and enjoy her caresses and to have sex until morning. Without any respect for marriage, she assured him that there was no fear of discovery, for "the man" is on a long journey, and by the moon she has calculated the date of his return." Proverbs 7:6–23.

This entire episode is laced with her tantalizing persuasions and many seducing compliments. Almost always there is a well plotted buildup before we yield to temptation. We don't fall into a trap and sin abruptly. We make seemingly innocent concessions, small allowances along the way, and then—not surprisingly—standards are eroded and defenses are down.

"Through the lattice I watched him follow her, like an animal heading for slaughter." Was there reluctance? Did he have some strange premonition? He seemed to me like a magnificent stag leaping toward a trap. Soon a razor-tipped arrow will pierce his vitals. I watch, stunned. This fine young man seems totally unaware of what this deadly choice will cost him. *The Message* renders Proverbs 7:23: "like a bird flying into the net, not knowing that its flying life is over."

Have you taken the time to carefully read this? How does it affect you? Is it not a stern warning for our men? Do you think it unmasks the beguiling face of temptation and shows us the vicious, devouring personality underneath?

> Now therefore, my sons, listen to me, and pay attention to the words of my mouth. Do not let your heart turn aside to her ways; Do not stray into her paths. For many are the victims she has cast down and numerous are her slain. Her house is the way to (hell) sheol, descending to the chambers of death.
>
> —Proverbs 7:24 NASB

How easy it is for us, women as well as men, to compromise when the allurement is so strong. We tell ourselves things such as, *Oh, I can safely do that,* or *All my friends are watching or reading this.*

So without consulting the Holy Spirit, we plunge headlong into movies, books, magazine articles, or other things that defile our spirits and cause our hearts to slide and grow cold toward Christ. These smaller compromises so often feed into the beginnings of illicit relationships.

John Phillips, a longtime friend and wonderful Christian husband and father, gave us excellent advice: "If you don't want to fall, don't walk where it's slippery."

During a low period in my Christian journey, I suffered from what Steve called "Friday night fever." I remember clearly a certain movie being raved about and having tremendous appeal. We were staying in a lovely resort hotel and Steve had seen the trailer on television in our room. His own decision was not to go, leaving me completely free. Accordingly, I joined two friends, and we went off to see the film.

When it was over, the three of us all felt the same. A defiling influence had reached out and affected us in such a way that each one felt sick at heart as we tumbled out of the theater into the crisp, snowy evening. We walked together and prayed. In time our spirits lifted, but it was a hard lesson.

I found a quotation in an old journal from *Jane Eyre* by Charlotte Bronte that I had copied many years ago. It's a difficult read, but so very penetrating.

That little space was given to delirious delusion.
I rested my temples on the breast of temptation
And put my neck voluntarily under her yoke of flowers.
I tasted her bitter cup. The pillow was burning,
There was an asp in the garland.
The wine has a bitter taste, her promises hollow; her offers false,
Within a year of twelve months, rapture would succeed to a lifetime
of regret.

"Why embrace the bosom of another man's wife? For a man's ways are in full view of the Lord, and He examines all his paths" (Proverbs 5:20 NIV).

All immoral paths, without exception, lead to destructive ends. Avoiding them is a lifelong discipline but has tangible and glorious rewards. Wonderfully, the blood of Christ is available for the cleansing of our past, and the conquering strength of Christ will be upon all who trust Him for the future.

What can I do to encourage you to immerse your minds in the scriptures? Let's read the book of Proverbs to our children in the daytime and to ourselves in the early morning and at night. These are the scrolls of life and should be unrolled in full view of our families. When we are exposed to wisdom's path, we are drawn to it with a wonderful magnetism. A holy and God-given reverence comes upon us to shun all other ways.

CHAPTER 13

SUBMISSION, THE BEAUTY
AND THE POWER

L ET'S EXPLORE TOGETHER what I believe to be a powerful
key of hammered gold.

The musical score of submission's dance was certainly not part of
my repertoire. Strong-willed, I tried to get my way in most situations. I
didn't do it aggressively; I was much more subtle than that. The language
of Christ's kingdom is so different from the language of our culture.

"In honor, prefer one another" (Romans 12:10).

"Esteem others as better than yourself" (Philippians 2:3).

"She that finds her life will lose it, but she that loses her life (for My
sake) will find it" (Matthew 10:39).

Jesus was determined that I come to know the path of life and
discover, in that path and in His presence, the fullness of joy. It has been
a long journey. Sometimes it feels as if I have only begun to understand
His ways. As I studied the biblical perspective in this regard, relating to
me as a woman, it was life-changing. The scriptures always are.

The introduction of the "S" word—submission—seems to bring
a reaction. This is totally expected in our current society. The tragedy
is that the biblical concept is sadly misunderstood and misconstrued.
I remember one darling girl, when she heard the word in class, was

sure it was a misprint! God has locked the key of submission into the foundational structure of the universe. It can unleash relationships into undreamed-of freedoms. Learning that dance, practicing it, and then really dancing will bring the sweet, refreshing rain of heaven down on you.

An Ancient War

An ancient war, a battle oft denied,
Swords that cut, and food to feed my heart of pride.
To please, yet strive to rule
A beloved one now of many years.
This struggle and the strain of it
Can flood my eyes with tears.

Incessant calls from deep inside,
His once so true and perfect bride.
The pull at times of keen desire,
Ignited as it were by fire,
To have dominion sure and clear,
So skilled now, that there is no fear,
To trample and offensive be.

Oh, God, please cause my eyes to see
This self-destructive bent in me,
My outstretched hand accepts the key
That will unlock those rooms so long debarred,
Bring healing to the heart I've scarred.

Steve has an arresting definition of the calling on men and women, husbands and wives: "Equal value, different roles."

The devil himself has worked hard to dehumanize us as women, to make us all objects, to degrade our nobility, our honor, our gifts, our high calling. It's not news that he has come to steal from us all we long for, all that is rightfully ours in a holy union and relationship. He has offered the sweet deserts of false power laced with lies, and he has seduced our minds to agree that competing and winning are everything.

He wants to make us believe that the expense of losing our lives for the advance of another is a waste, which is the opposite of what Jesus taught. His subtle brilliance has led us to believe that the external is paramount and the spirit can survive on what's left behind when the party is over and the beer is gone.

If there is a key that will unlock a room of unequalled treasure and value in marriage, the devil's plan is to hide that key, or at least make it look like something it was never meant to be.

"Who can find a virtuous woman for her price [value] is far above rubies" (Proverbs 31:10).

You will remember that the word *value* in the Hebrew mind and language is rooted in surrender. Hang on to that word as we proceed. Let's cleanse our palates of all other flavors with this scripture before we advance to the study of this controversial word: *submission.*

The Greek word *hypotaso* occurs forty-nine times in thirty-two verses in the New Testament, and is variously translated as "subject, subjection, obedience, submission."

Greek: *Hypotaso*—to be under obedience, to subdue unto, to put under, to be subject, to submit self to.

(Notice that all of the above definitions engage the will.)

The Greek meaning is to come under quietly, (no huffing, no puffing) to fall in with, (no holding back, but go to meet), a certain eagerness.

Let's take one of the above elements and go to the Oxford Dictionary: "To subordinate"—secondary, next, below, depending on, coming in place or time after.

Jesus Christ, our supreme example, leads the way. He consistently walked in submission to His Father's will and in obedience to His own earthly parents. This was His lifestyle, His deliberate and highest choice.

"And He went down with them and came to Nazareth and he continued in subjection to them; and his mother treasured all these things in her heart. And Jesus kept increasing in wisdom and stature and in favor with God and man" (Luke 2:51–52).

Greek: *Wisdom* (Jesus increased in wisdom) denotes practical skill and acumen.

Favor—the divine influence upon the heart and its reflection in the life, including cheerful and grateful.

In an act of pure humility, "Jesus rose from supper and took off his outer garments, and taking a servant's towel, He fastened it around his waist. Then He poured water into the wash basin and began to wash the disciple's feet and to wipe them with the servant's towel with which He was girded" (John 13:4–5).

Now follow Jesus into the lonely garden of Gethsemane with your keenest imagination.

"And going a little farther, He threw himself on the ground on his face and prayed saying, 'My Father, if it is possible, let this cup pass away from me: nevertheless not what I will [not what I desire] but what you will and desire'" (Matthew 26:39).

Find yourself a hollow in the ground or lean against one of those gnarled olive trees. Know your heart to break and pour out like water as you glimpse His posture, His anguish. Do remember, He went the full distance of surrender to the Father's will—all for you, all for me.

How did we get it so wrong? It seems we have utterly reversed what Jesus lived and taught. "And whoever desires to be first among you must be your slave. Just as the Son of Man came not to be waited on, but to serve, and to give His life as a ransom for many [the price paid to set them free]" (Matthew 20:27–28).

Who in contemporary culture would dream that to be the servant is the noblest of roles? So it must be true after all, that when the curtains

SUBMISSION, THE BEAUTY AND THE POWER

open on eternity, those we expected to be first will be last, and those we expected to be last will be first.

"And behold, there are some [now] last who will be first [then], and there are some [now] first who will be last [then]" (Luke 13:30).

All of Christ's earthly life was lived out in full obedience to the Father and dependence upon Him. Why was this so? Because He was always God but was revealed to humanity in flesh and blood. Can we accept that He lived this life of reliance, at least in part, to show us the path of life by example? His words in John's gospel account attest to this.

"That I do nothing of myself [of my own accord], or on my own authority, but I say exactly what my Father has taught me....For I always do what pleases Him [the Father]" (John 8:28–29).

The relationship Christ had with his Father is the same relationship that Christ intends for us to experience and enjoy with Him. "Apart from me [cut off from vital union with me] you can do nothing" (John 15:5).

The Holy Spirit uses the same Greek word, *hypotaso*, in two letters to young churches:

Wives be subject [be submissive and adapt yourselves] to your own husbands as [a service] to the Lord. For the husband is the head of the wife as Christ is head of the church, Himself the Savior of [His] body. As the church is subject to Christ, so let wives also be subject in everything to their husbands.

—Ephesians 5:22–24

Wives be subject to your husbands [subordinate and adapt yourselves to them], as is right and fitting and your proper duty in the Lord.

—Colossians 3:18–19

Both of these scriptures are accompanied by demanding directives to the men.

Beauty and submission interlock. This brings us to the question: Can we be truly beautiful without a submissive spirit? Conversely: Is it possible to be submissive in spirit and not be utterly beautiful? Do we really believe that we can know and experience the true value of one without the other?

We can, amazingly, beautify ourselves in this highest of independent choices by being in submission. It is a well-controlled decision of the will to dispose myself into a stance of submission, to place myself deliberately under my husband. To do this well is to do so with Christ's enabling. Here is the capstone scripture to give us clear insight into the divine weaving of this powerful principle into the tapestry of relationships.

"But I want you to know and realize that Christ is the head of every man, the head of a woman is her husband, and the head of Christ is God" (1 Corinthians 11:3).

It needs to be understood that both the husband and the wife are in submission, she to her husband (for Christ's sake) and he to Christ. St.Paul's view was that the husband's headship would be a spiritual role of leadership, both sacrifical and selfless.

Perhaps you are single—or a widow. If that is the case, I encourage you to quickly find some godly umbrella of protection in a brother or close friend as a safe reference point for accountability and shelter. Let the Holy Spirit teach and lead you.

Scripture teaches us that women are born for palaces. So, tell me why, when we were called to such tremendous nobility ourselves, would we usurp an oversized crown by seizing the God-ordained authority given to our husbands? "The King's daughter in the inner part of the palace is all glorious; her clothing is wrought in gold" (Psalm 45:13).

Contrary to misguided opinions, for us to defiantly resist and—perhaps not so defiantly—deliberately duck and skirt around this principle is useless if not eventually fatal. If we persist on such a path, we will find that we have demolished the divine framework designed to give us the shelter and joy we crave.

Kings' daughters are among your honorable women: at your right hand stands the Queen in gold of Ophir. So will the King desire your beauty, because he is your Lord be submissive and reverence and honor him, and oh daughter of Tyre, the richest of the people shall entreat your favor with a gift.

—Psalm 45:9

A Fool to Rule

It seemed so right to have my way,
My point so strong, what could he say
To intersect my heady path?
Though somewhere there I stirred his wrath,
And yet he seemed so kind, benign,
A gentleman so well defined.
So I pushed him here and pressed him there,
I lived my life with personal flair,
Until one day he distant seemed,
Further apart than we'd ever dreamed.

I vaguely wondered, had I lost his heart
That beat for me in every part?
I continued firm in my headstrong way,
I chose my path and led the way.
He stepped aside, made way for me,
So stuck was I, I could not see
The drift of one on a shifting sea.

Confused, I struggled now to cope,
I fought and scrambled, gasped for hope,
To span the gulf now formed by years,
This space between us fed my fears.

God, tell me true, did I do wrong?
Did I stomp on his heart, did I smother his song?
Now I am all forlorn, alone,
Is there still time to bring me home?

"Every wise woman builds her house, but the foolish one tears it down with her own hands" (Proverbs 14:1).

CHAPTER 14

WINNING THE HEART

OF A KING

TWO FAMOUS WOMEN, both breathtaking and chosen above all others, rose to be crowned queen in the most powerful kingdom of their age. Each married the king and retained her own will. Queen Vashti fell into disfavor, lost her crown, and was banished; but Queen Esther found favor and kept hers.

This drama is colorfully depicted in the first chapter of the book of Esther. King Ahasuerus (Xerxes) is the reigning monarch. He rules over 127 provinces from India to Ethiopia. His royal throne is in the palace at Shushan, the capital of the Persian Empire.

This powerful king throws a lavish party for his princes and all the chief officers in the Persian army. He also invites the nobles and governors of the provinces under his domain.

This party of all parties, marked by rich feasting and much liberal drinking, lasted a total of 180 days. The extravaganza culminated when the king issued an invitation to the remaining citizens—everyone resident in the capital city of Shushan, both small and great. This turned into a seven-day feast in the court garden of the king's palace. Scripture goes into great detail describing the setting: fine white cloth hangings with additional colors of blue and green; sweeping and elegant curtains fastened with fine linen and purple cords to silver rings on marble pillars. Our eyes are wide and we are flooded with anticipation.

Grand couches of both silver and gold rest on mosaic pavement of porphyry, white marble, mother of pearl, and precious colored stones. Each of the golden goblets for drinking wine is unique. The royal wine is generously available to all, although no one is compelled to drink. Each guest was to receive whatever he wished.

While the king's celebration is in full swing, Queen Vashti is giving a banquet in the royal house for all the noble women of Shushan.

On the seventh day, being full of wine and merriment, the king was casting around in his mind for a grand finale. Perhaps there was some boredom among the guests, and he needed an elaborate culmination to climax this seemingly endless display of wealth and prosperity. Ahasuerus thought, *Ah, Vashti, magnificent Vashti, the power of her beauty will stir them all.*

Accordingly, he commanded his seven eunuchs to bring her before him so he could show her off. Her response enraged the king. Vashti refused to come. The Hebrew use of this word tells us that hers was no weak or pleading refusal. She refused utterly. There are various opinions as to the request of Ahasuerus, some of which line up in definite sympathy for Vashti. As this is not a novel, we will choose to stay with the text and seek to learn from it. Without a doubt, this outlandish party in Persia took a new twist.

Burning with anger, the king sought the immediate counsel of his senior advisors—seven wise princes. "What is to be done to Queen Vashti because of her refusal?"

Prince Memucan gave a direct and clear answer to the King:

Vashti has not only done wrong to the king but also to all the princes and to all the peoples who are in all the provinces of King Ahasuerus, for this deed of the queen will become known to all women, making their husbands contemptible in their eyes. This very day the ladies of Persia and Media who have heard of the queen's behavior will be telling it to all the king's princes. So contempt and wrath in plenty will arise.

—Esther 1:16, 18

Note the ripple effect of a single refusal: excessive contempt, anger, disrespect, and discord are predicted by Memucan. Here, again, we find the Holy Spirit teaches through contrast.

Hebrew: *Disrespect*—dis-esteem, disdain, scorn

Oxford Dictionary: *Dis-esteem*—opposite of "thinking highly of."

Characteristics of Disrespect

Not gentle	Saucy	Impertinent
Unrestrained	Intrusive [forcing oneself in]	
Startling	Offensive	Out of place
Sudden	Aggressive	Unsympathetic
Abrupt	Repulsive	Insulting
Insolent	Cold	Offering resistance

Memucan continued with his advice. (See Esther 1:19–20 NKJV.) In short, his solution was that Vashti was to come no more before the king, and her royal position was to go to another. As a result, all wives would honor their husbands both great and small.

Hebrew: *Honor*—value, dignity.

Memucan's advice pleased the king, and he dispatched letters to all his provinces instructing that "every man should rule in his own house."

The kingdom of Persia was then without a queen. The solution was to gather lovely virgins from all 127 provinces and, from this vast selection, the maiden that pleased the king would be queen instead of Vashti.

This is where Esther, a distinguished young woman, enters the story. Esther was a captive in a foreign land. In many simple ways each day she was being prepared to win the heart of the king.

> And Mordecai brought up Hadassah, that is, Esther, his uncle's daughter, for she had neither father nor mother. The young woman was lovely and beautiful. When her mother and father died, Mordecai took her as his own daughter.
>
> —Esther 2:7

I believe her "crown" was being formed when she was a young girl. She had allowed her character to be molded in inward beauty. How did she learn such a profound level of respect and obedience, all couched in wisdom beyond her years? The maturing process of a resilient and submissive spirit had begun long before she entered the palace.

Without a mother there would be much to care for domestically. Undoubtedly, she was tempted at times to fuss and make a scene at Mordecai's instructions. Of one thing I am certain: Esther was respectful and obedient in the smallest details of life. How do I know this? You don't learn these strong character qualities overnight. The big tests of obedience and submission were still to come. When Esther's test came, she didn't fail; instead, by God's grace, she passed with flying colors!

Although God is not mentioned in the entire book of Esther, it is crystal clear that she was schooled by Mordecai in awe and reverence for the Lord God of her fathers and that she had learned to honor her adoptive cousin's legitimate authority. As she moved out into independence in the big, wide world and competed to be queen, her early training commended her to Hegai. Suitably, he was the eunuch in charge of the harem. Esther's obedient spirit and restrained demeanor won her unprecedented favor during the long months of preparation.

> And the maiden pleased Hegai and obtained his favor. And he speedily gave her the things for her purification and her portion of food and the seven chosen maidens to be given her from the King's palace; and he removed her and her maids to the best [apartment] in the harem.
>
> —Esther 2:9

The next instruction she obeyed came from Mordecai. "Esther had not made known her nationality or her kindred, for Mordecai had instructeded her not to do so" (Esther 2:10).

In competition with all the beauties in the land to be queen over the world's largest empire, Esther left the old cousin behind, outside the palace walls. What would he know? What did she care? She could have been so consumed with her newfound independence, but there was a trait in her character that was dancing its way to the king's heart.

As each maiden's turn came to go in to the king, she was given whatever she desired. Can you imagine the long hall-ways of gowns, the chests of accessories, the jewelry, the in-house squabbling? Here was a time to creatively express herself—the choice of cloth and of color, the lavish, the elegant, the classic. *What shall I wear?* "She requested nothing but what Hegai, the king's chamberlain, the keeper of women, appointed or advised" (Esther 2:15).

What was the result when she was all dressed and ready to go to meet the king? "And Esther won favor in the sight of all who saw her" (Esther 2:15). And she was off to the royal palace.

How would the king respond? "And the King loved Esther more than all the women and she obtained grace and favor in his sight more than all the virgins. So he set a royal crown upon her head and made her Queen instead of Vashti" (Esther 2:17).

Hebrew: *Grace*—kindness, precious, well favored, objective beauty.

Hebrew: *Favor*—loving kindness, mercy, pity (as if to bow the neck only in courtesy to an equal).

Now all of the virgins were stunningly beautiful; they would not have been chosen otherwise. What was it about Esther that made the king fall in love with her? Of course, her beauty was a contributing factor. The choice in dress would please him; Hegai would be sensitive to the king's taste. Ultimately and finally it was without a doubt the power and magnetism of her spirit. This was not produced on demand but carefully cultivated through a long history of highest choices, some of them both costly and painful.

Do you know what a "submissive spirit" brings out in a man, young or old?

- A desire to protect and cherish
- A desire to be honorable as befits a prince or king
- Tenderness and all those qualities that women long for

We don't get our "rights" by clamoring and demanding. Esther was given half the kingdom. This is how the Almighty has set it up in the universe. Headship and submission, as found in the scriptures, are of the nature that evokes these protective qualities in a man, and should develop hugely sacrificial devotion on his part!

Esther is now queen of the entire realm of the Medes and Persians. Does she forget about her old guardian? Does pride of position consume her so that she spurns his wisdom and advice, his sandals, and his homely robe? Does she assume her "rights" to independence after all, severing that deference and respect? No! "For Esther did what Mordecai told her, as she had done under his care" (Esther 2:20).

The greatest test is yet to come. Palace intrigue thickens as a wicked counselor, Haman, is promoted above the other princes. All are to bow and give him homage. They do bow, with the exception of Mordecai. He had openly revealed his origins as a Jew and would bow to no man but to God alone. Haman is so filled with rage that he plots to kill not just Mordecai, but all the Jews in the kingdom.

With manipulation and lies he causes the king to decree and irrevocably seal the wholesale destruction of the Jews. Under Haman's crafty sculpting of the orders, all Jews are to be killed on a set day in the month of Adar, and their possessions are to be seized.

Loud and bitter wailing fills the air above the city of Shushan. Mordecai tears his clothes and puts on sackcloth and ashes. In Persian culture this was the outward symbol of sorrow, mourning, and distress. He sends a copy of the edict to Esther, now writhing in anguish for her people. He tells her to go to the king and plead for their lives. Esther advises Mordecai that to come to the king without being summoned means certain death except when he holds out his golden scepter. In the busyness of the kingdom, she had not been summoned for thirty days. Mordecai warns:

Do not imagine that you in the king's palace can escape more than all the Jews. For if you remain silent at this time, relief and deliverance will arise for the Jews from another place and you and your father's house will perish. And who knows whether you have not attained royalty for such a time as this?

—Esther 4:13–14

Now comes the challenge to nobility and sacrifice. Esther immediately galvanizes into action. God loves this sort of obedience. Esther instructs Mordecai: "Go assemble all the Jews who are found in Shushan and fast for me. Do not eat or drink for three days, night or day. I and my maidens will also fast in the same way. And thus I will go to the king which is not according to the law; and if I perish, I perish" (Esther 4:16). So with great courage:

Now it came about on the third day that Esther put on her royal robes and stood in the inner court of the king's palace in front of the king's rooms, and the king was sitting on his royal throne in the throne room, opposite the entrance to the palace.

And it happened when the king saw Esther the queen standing in the court, she obtained favor in his sight; and the king extended to Esther the golden scepter which was in his hand. So Esther came near and touched the top of the scepter.

Then the king said to her, "What is troubling you, Queen Esther? And what is your request? Even to half of the kingdom it will be given you"

—Esther 5:1–3 NASB

Queen Esther has a discreet plan to thwart the king's decree. She throws two banquets, inviting only the king and wicked Haman to join her. At the first banquet she withholds her request and obviously highly stimulates her husband's curiosity. Her elegant hospitality only serves to inflate Haman and accentuate his destructive pride and hatred.

He recounts his glory to his wife and friends, even describing the queen's exclusive invitation. Yet all of this does not satisfy his insatiable craving for power. Mordecai's failure to bow to him at the king's gate gnaws at his innards and spoils everything. Accordingly, Haman's wife and friends advise him to have a gallows built, fifty cubits high, and ask the king to have Mordecai hung on it.

God's sovereign plan and immediate powerful presence foil this vicious plot. That night, amazingly, the king could not sleep, so he gave orders to have the book of records read to him. As God would have it, they read to him of how Mordecai had reported two guards who plotted to assassinate the king. Hearing of this loyal act, the king asked if there had been any honor given to Mordecai.

Who should approach the royal chamber next but Haman, looking for permission to hang his enemy. The king speaks first, "Tell me, Haman, what should be done for the one whom the king desires to honor?"

Haman is so sure of himself, he thinks, *This must be me.* Thus he advises the king as to what is in his heart for himself: "Let them bring a royal robe which the king has worn and a horse on which the king has ridden, on whose head a royal crown has been placed. Let the robe and horse be handed over to one of the king's noble princes and let them array the man whom the king delights to honor and lead him on horseback through the city square and proclaim, 'Thus it shall be done to the man whom the king desires to honor.'"

To Haman's abject horror, the king commands he do exactly this for Mordecai the Jew.

In spite of his humiliation, Haman must now appear at Esther's second banquet.

While wine was being served, the king said again to Esther, "What is your petition, Queen Esther? It shall be granted. And what is your request? Even to half of the kingdom it shall be performed." Then Queen Esther said, "If I have found favor in your sight, O king, and if it pleases the king, let my life be given me at my petition and my people at my request; for we are sold, I and my people, to be destroyed, slain, and wiped out of existence!" … Then King Ahasuerus said to Queen Esther, "Who is he, and where is he, who dares presume in his heart to do that?" And Esther said, "An adversary and an enemy, even this wicked Haman." Then Haman was afraid before the king and queen.

—Esther 7:2–7

The story concludes with Haman being hung, Esther being favored, and, although the edict cannot be changed, the Jews are allowed to arm and defend themselves when the fateful day comes. Mordecai, in his quiet wisdom, is promoted to first minister and receives Haman's estate as a bounty.

The city of Shushan rings with shouts of rejoicing. The air is electrified for there is joy and gladness and honor for the Jews. Esther's submissive spirit is rewarded with regal authority. At her command, two days were set aside every year for her people to celebrate and to send gifts to the poor. Even today, Jewish people around the world celebrate the feast of Purim in honor of Esther and in memory of these startling events.

Now that we have followed the life of this lovely young queen and observed the power of her spirit to win the heart of the king, it would be totally unfair not to address the role of the husband, who is so clearly instructed in the Word of God.

It may surprise some men to known that their feet are to walk in a path far more stringent than ours as they relate to their wives. I remember years ago hearing Dr. Stephen Olford, an outstanding Christian Bible teacher from England, speak about these things. He taught that if men really want to understand their biblical mandate, they must follow Christ to His cross. There they will view the level to which they are to go in laying down their lives.

Carefully observe that these next two scriptures are about obedience by the husband. Let's remember that he needs to grow, too, and we water that by prayer. His growth is always enhanced by our expressions of appreciation and respect. In this area it might be wise to let the Lord supervise his growth and avoid the danger of interfering with the process!

"Husbands, love your wives, as Christ loved the church and gave Himself up for her" (Ephesians 5:25).

"Even so husbands should love their wives as (being in a sense) their own bodies. He who loves his own wife loves himself. For no man ever hated his own flesh, but nourishes and cherishes it, as Christ does the church" (Ephesians 5:28–29).

Sometimes it's so hard to bring the ends together and tie them in a love knot. What do I mean by that? On one hand, this gorgeous male you fell head-over-heels in love with appears dominant, sometimes aggressive, and even loses his temper. Everything in you wants to rise up, mount your high horse, and tell him off well and truly. At the same time, you both crave peace and harmony. The secret is to always be willing to say those two words that are so deeply locked away and difficult to bring to the surface: "I'm sorry."

More and more, we see that this can be a beautiful dance, listening to each other's hearts, and not just the spoken words. You may have a lot of fun learning the difference between these two.

I've heard some women say, "If only my husband would behave the way the Bible instructs, then I could easily submit to him."

Knowing what some wives cope with, I can heartily agree. On the other hand, I believe that if wives will begin to express genuine respect for some aspect of their husband's person, they will discover some positive response and some movement in that heart of stone. This is miraculous!

Wendy poured out her woes to me regarding her husband's verbal cruelties. At such times we always prayed and asked the Holy Spirit for insight together, because everyone's marriage relationship is unique.

"What first attracted you to your husband?" I asked.

"His looks; he was so handsome."

I asked her when she last admired him and told him so. There was no answer for that, but she became very excited at the possibility. "That's the best advice I've had for a long time," she bubbled.

Did everything get better overnight? No. The way was hard, and it was to be a long road.

The journey of a tiny apple seed may seem interminable until, one day, you hold in your own hands that delicious, ripe fruit. Have patience. It really will happen. There will be a response. When scripture tells us in Ephesians 5:33 to admire (Greek: esteem, honor, notice, appreciate, prize, and adore) our husbands, there is a reason. And if he discourages us, we persevere and hold onto the encouragement in 1 Corinthians 13, "Love never fails."

CHAPTER 15

MY BEAUTIFUL BREASTS:
EXCLUSIVE SPRINGS

Do you know the saying, "Drink from your own rain barrel, draw water from your own spring-fed well?" It's true. Otherwise you may one day come home and find your barrel empty and your well polluted. Your spring water is for you and for you only, not to be passed around among strangers. Bless your fresh-flowing fountain! Enjoy the wife you married as a young man....Don't ever quit taking delight in her body. Never take her love for granted!

—Proverbs 5:15–18 TM

THE ABOVE INSTRUCTIONS—FROM a father to his son—give us insight into our role as women.

This scripture was written in the Middle East where water is a precious and a sometimes scarce commodity. Cisterns and holding places for water collected the precious liquid when it rained. Water is essential to life. We can live extended days without food, but only three days without water. A good householder always maintained an uncracked and unbroken cistern.

How does this crucial picture transfer to our marriages? There are two answers: we are to be refreshing and accessible, and then our "refreshment" is to be for our husbands and for none other. Our thirsty husbands should not need to look anywhere else for satisfaction. Sometimes we drop the ball in this area, but it is tremendous fun to work at being a refreshing wife. We keep an emotional reserve for our husbands by preparing ourselves mentally, physically, and emotionally for their return.

For me it can be a discipline not to dissipate my precious reserve on the far-extended fringes of friendship. Sometimes our "girl-time," our lunches out, and our long coffees get our best, while our husbands are left with what remains at the end of the day. I have to admit from personal experience that sometimes it's the "frayed ends."

Let's make it a goal to look and be our absolute physical best when he walks in. I don't mean wearing a ballroom gown, but do make a big effort here. You'll enjoy it, and so will he. Let's not use the I-don't-have-time excuse, because we do find the time if we want to. It will be worth it all to see your man's eyes begin to sparkle with admiration.

So much works against us in our quest to keep refreshing springs for our husbands. It takes little to pollute a well or a spring.

We were in Romania one very hot summer. Many days the temperature was close to a hundred degrees. For two weeks, Steve and a Christian translator visited a large number of village homes, bringing New Testaments and beautifully printed children's picture Bibles. There were opportunities to hear their stories, to share the love of Christ, and sometimes to pray with whole households. Translation is not regarded as an impediment to friendship in Romania; there are twelve official languages within this ancient country.

Exhausted from a morning in the heat, the two men lowered a bucket into the village well. Not their bucket, and not their well! A local lady who was passing by started to yell. They tried to ignore her because their thirst was overwhelming! This moved the yelling up to screaming and screeching. Why are these people suddenly so hostile? When it was all translated, it transpired that a cat, alas, had fallen into the well two weeks before and drowned. She was desperate to prevent them from poisoning themselves!

The apostle Paul warns us against inward pollution:

"Dearly beloved, let us cleanse ourselves from all filthiness of the flesh and spirit, perfecting holiness in the fear of God" (2 Corinthians 7:1).

"Rather we have renounced secret and shameful ways" (2 Corinthians 4:2 NIV).

Let's guard ourselves from the leisure of that steamy novel, those triangular affairs on TV, and those illicit scenes in movies. Why? Because our unsuspecting hearts are so easily caught off guard and drawn in, especially when we are tired. Keep in mind that the green grass across the fence will always call us. How quickly comparisons kick in, and in our minds we can cross the boundaries.

"My husband, bless him, just doesn't measure up to that handsome hulk on the silver screen." So soon and so easily we discover that our hearts are adrift.

Jude Bateman, a wonderful friend, intense and passionate for Jesus commented, "If we make a small concession, it can change our direction, even if it is just by one degree!"

Here is a story from another dear and honest friend in her own words:

Before the family went on a holiday one summer, I was given a book by my mother-in-law. I needed something to read, but I could feel the Holy Spirit telling me that I shouldn't be reading that book. I didn't realize the danger, and I had no idea of the effect it would have. It was well written, hard to put down, and very intertwined.

My husband and I weren't doing well at the time. I read it, finished it, and ended up almost walking into an affair with a man who was also on holiday. The allure and fantasy of this book was feeding my emotions. When this guy fed me compliments, it was an escape. All of a sudden, the fantasy presented itself. Already my defenses were whittled down with the effect of the book. I did not have a whole lot of strength. Here was a live flesh presentation just a few cabins away.

I never thought of the book until several weeks later. Then it all connected—how I had opened the door. By God's grace I chose to escape, and by the goodness of the Holy Spirit, I have refused since that time to read anything that brings me down those paths. I don't know when I'm vulnerable, and it doesn't take much to fan the wrong flame.

What our gracious heavenly Father actually intended for our deepest satisfaction and delight was that our husbands should have exclusive access beneath our blouses, and that this and what follows should be a thrill beyond comparison to both of us, without being marred by the guilt and regrets of muddied streams!

"Let your fountain be blessed, And rejoice with the wife of your youth. As a loving deer and a graceful doe, Let her breasts satisfy you at all times; And always be enraptured with her love" (Proverbs 5:18–19 NKJV).

Here we have delightful word pictures that describe us, so we want to explore the Hebrew meaning of *loving* and *graceful*.

Hebrew: *Loving*—to have affection (sexually or otherwise), to be loved, to be lovely, to be a lover, like a friend.

Hebrew: *Graceful*—gracious, kind, pleasant.

Stop and ask the Holy Spirit to give you the creativity and inspiration that will be unique for your relationship with your husband. Decide to walk in obedience to these gentle instructions.

Our husbands are instructed to "Enjoy life with the woman whom you love all the days of your fleeting life which He has given you under the sun; for this is your reward in life and in your toil in which you have labored under the sun" (Ecclesiastes 9:9 NASB).

What about our breasts? "May her breasts satisfy you always." They are a gift to us as women; a gift that we may give generously and lavishly, but with exclusivity, to our own husbands. This does not mean we must bind them up to flatness in public but that we both honor and cherish this gift and not expose our two fawns (called "the twins of a gazelle" in Song of Songs) inappropriately to those who pass by without covenant or ownership. You say "Okay, Trish. You're getting a bit heavy here." Not a bit!

Firstly, *covenant* is what you entered into with a combination of sacred vows and sexual union. Ownership of your breasts and mine is clearly delineated by St. Paul.

"The wife does not have authority over her own body, but the husband does; and likewise also the husband does not have authority over his own body, but the wife does" (1 Corinthians 7:4 NASB).

This mutual reciprocity would have been totally counter-cultural in St Paul's day!

Hebrew: *Breasts*—as the seat of love or from its (love's) shape.

By the way, I find this absolutely exquisite as to the sacredness and loveliness of this part of our bodies. I never cease to be amazed at their effect on my husband. The scriptural term is that our breasts have the power to intoxicate. This is a sublime mystery.

The Hebrew term used in "let her breasts satisfy you at all times" means to slake the thirst, to make drunk, to take (his) fill, to satiate. Similarly, "Be exhilarated always with her love" carries the meaning of ravished, enraptured, and intoxicated.

So let me ask, "Do we intoxicate our husbands? Is he—that wonderful man you chose to marry—exhilarated? When last did you observe with fully legitimate pleasure that he was enraptured with you, with your bust?" This is entirely possible. This is to be expected and desired. This is your God-given loveliness. This is the biblical benchmark.

Take time then to be lovely. Don't focus on what you may feel are imperfections. Be excited about him and about preparing yourself for him. "A bundle of myrrh is my beloved to me that lies all night between my breasts" (Song of Songs 1:13 KJV).

This excellence of combined beauty and emotion is not random because it is inspired by the Holy Spirit to give instruction and even correction. Believe me, in my own marriage this verse has been both. As passionately and deeply as I love and adore Steve, I'm not always readily available to him. My needs, my feelings, my will, my weariness, one and all, or combinations of them, can become the reins that pull me back from being lovingly accessible. Maybe I should think more seriously about the priorities, time, and energy of my days.

So much is involved in our minds and our wills. It is shocking to discover that *how we think* can change our moods. If our feelings and weariness are both putting us in a mood to avoid making love, then it will be the last thing we feel like doing. Yet if we consider the invitation in the Word to be available, our feelings do change and weariness flies away as well. Amazing.

I love Stormie Omartian's suggestion, "When your husband wants to make love, ask for a few minutes to prepare yourself."

Let's unpack the last exploding secret that will bring wonder and joy.

Hebrew: *Myrrh*—a bitter herb, its usage is to do with bitterness, the distilling out of bitterness.

This is a great wonder and beauty. The accumulated bitterness in his person, the angry boss, the lost sale, the unsavory assaults to his eyes and mind, all the ragged stresses of the day, are distilled out in the very act of making love and being held. A man should find in his wife a place of refuge and shelter. He discovers that, in her eager love, bitterness is distilled into one of life's costliest perfumes.

CHAPTER 16

DRESS THE KING'S DAUGHTER

"Her clothing is fine linen and purple"
—Proverbs 31:22 NASB

WILL I HAVE princess sheets on my bed, Nana?" This was the spontaneous question from our darling four-year-old granddaughter, who was anticipating her first night at our new home. With petite features and a ready smile, she loves us both, loves to paint, to play, and to feed horses when we walk. Above all else, she loves pretty dresses and beads and sparkles in her hair, dressing up, and then dressing up again. Furthermore, her brother, our grandson, both deep-spirited and boisterous, loves an outfit, so long as there is a sword with it to stick in his belt!

Why is it that little ones are so absorbed in this, yet as we grow up—with the exception of weddings or special occasions—we tend to lapse in this area?

The subject of dress is sensitive and delicate. I don't want to offend, and I don't want to judge, but neither do any of us want to be the "gray dressers." Let's just put the subject on the table and think about it together.

The Bible gives us a key that will unlock the closet of the princess. Inner personal beauty can be likened to a valuable artistic painting. For my birthday years ago, I was given a now well-loved print by Robert Bateman called "The Watch." I did not tack it to the wall just as it was with a couple of rusty nails. It was stunning in its near perfection, and it needed to be well set. I took it to Walshes Gallery, where a highly skilled lady framed it tastefully. Mrs. Walsh herself chose a charcoal frame and two shades of matting to bring out the colors in the picture. We have all seen what a difference a well-selected frame makes to a picture. Let us think of the "frame" as our outer life. How do we present God's creative work? Why not do the best we can with His masterpiece? All of us have a fundamental need to be admired. Men are most certainly affected by what they see. To be appropriately and carefully dressed can evoke in our husbands the appreciation we have need of. You have been gifted with feminine qualities. Listen, you are beautiful. Cultivate your femininity, accent it, and have fun doing so. Studying this whole area, both biblically and culturally, gave me the courage to ask three different men for their opinions.

The following are the points of view on dress from three men in my life.

Steve: "When your husband sees you standing and talking with a group of ladies, you should stand out as supremely feminine and desirable."

Here's the scale from his viewpoint:

Barely Feminine	More Feminine	Increasingly Feminine	More Feminine Than Them All!
Sweats	Jeans	Skirt	Dress
Rugby Shirt	Top	Blouse	
Pink Socks			

Steve says, "If you move along the scale one notch to the right, you increase your feminine appearance. You can look smart at any stage. I think that dress blends with poise and dignity."

Geoff: I remember two occasions during our son Geoff's late teens and early twenties that I phoned and asked him to give me his view on the way girls and women should dress. To my surprise, he didn't even hesitate in giving me his assessment: "Dress appropriately. Dress to look good but not seductive. It's almost an intangible. I can't describe exactly what appropriate is, but you know when it's inappropriate. Dress with appropriate sexiness, but not salaciously (Webster's Dictionary: leading to indulge in lust.) If women are honest, they know where the line is. If they don't know, that's why they come to your class! You don't want other men to think of you in a sexual way at all. You are to be attractive without being suggestive. Dressing attractively says a lot about who you are without you saying anything. If someone is in sweats and no makeup, you know she didn't put any effort into the day."

Geoff went on to say: "In terms of finding and maintaining a mate, even if you're not a knockout, people will be drawn to you if you take care. It's important to accent feminine qualities in a discreet way. It's good for you and good for your partner because he feels good about you. If you are married and let it slide, you are asking for problems. If you don't maintain yourself, neither will your husband. If you make a lot of effort and you're not complimented, then say, 'I did this for you, and you didn't notice. I felt unnoticed.' It doesn't cost a lot to dress nicely.

"There are always a lot of striking women, but if the one he's chosen does everything she can to make herself attractive, he will be more than proud. If you don't, he'll be embarrassed, but he won't say anything. This goes for everything from clothes to weight. You need to give him a visual reason to stay at home."

Jeff: Jeff is our fine son-in-law. His response was, "Dignity is appropriate. If you want to be treated like a woman of dignity, a good place to start is to dress like one."

For several years the "Rubies" studies ran in Vancouver for twelve weeks consecutively. We always invited the girls to visit the Bentall Centre building or the Pacific Centre Mall in downtown Vancouver during the noon hour. They were to pack a picnic and find a comfortable place to be, and then watch the women come streaming out of their various offices on their lunch breaks. They were to notice how they dressed. They found that the majority of them looked great and seemed to be accenting their feminine qualities.

Consider that after being surrounded all day by ladies who look like ladies, a husband comes home to his wife, who hasn't done her hair and is wearing sweats. She has not put on any makeup and has made no effort with her appearance. Wherever our husbands go, whether they are cab drivers, lawyers, couriers, financial advisors, or waiters, they will see women who have taken care with their appearance. So let's get with it and spend at least a little time on looking our best. It makes his arrival at home a pleasant event rather than a continuation of the day's drudgery.

Study yourself and your body language in sweats. Even the way you sit changes when you wear a skirt or dress, and the way you feel about yourself may change as well. Appearance is, of course, not the most important aspect of our lives, but think about it and consider it carefully.

You have prepared a favorite and special meal for your family. How do you present it? After all the hard work, do you go for paper plates and plastic knives and forks, or do you bring out linen and china to bring dignity and an almost elusive significance to the meal?

One lady, after taking the class on appearance, went home and asked her husband how he would like for her to dress. She wanted him to think about his answer. He didn't even hesitate. He told her which clothes he liked and which ones to get rid of and replace. What woman doesn't want to hear "Go shopping, girl" from her husband?

Another woman complained, "My husband wants me to wear high heels when he takes me out. Can you imagine how hard it is to get into a pickup truck when I'm wearing heels?" I wanted to tell her that most women would love it if their husbands noticed what they wear and wanted them to dress up for a night on the town.

Ask your husband what he likes and doesn't like. Dare to take him shopping. And by the way, when your husband buys you something to wear—that's right—wear it, even if you need to dress it up.

Here comes another confession from me. I am extremely independent-minded when it comes to my personal choice of clothes. I didn't dream of including Steve or even asking his opinion. Steve, on the other hand, was too much of a gentleman to interfere. I wanted him to appreciate and applaud my choices.

Occasionally he would buy me something and surprise me. I don't remember exactly how it came about, but once we were shopping together, and he was having fun looking through the racks. The long and short of it is that he chose some clothes for me that always get the compliments: "I sure love your suit, Trisha."

Later, while I was buried inside the store, he came in waving an elegant, three-piece Portuguese dress, full length, in a dusty yellow. It was on a street rack, drastically reduced, and perfect for more formal occasions. I've discovered after all these years that he has great taste and knows what looks good on me.

Just in case you were wondering what God thinks about all this, according to the following passage from the Old Testament, He does not disapprove of us looking amazing:

> Then I washed you with water … and I anointed you with oil. I clothed you also with embroidered cloth, and shod you with [fine seal] leather, and I girded you about with fine linen, and I covered you with silk. I decked you also with ornaments, and I put bracelets on your wrists and a chain on your neck. And I put a ring on your nostril and earrings in your ears, and a beautiful crown upon your head….And you were exceedingly beautiful, and you prospered into royal estate.
> —Ezekiel 16:9–15

Let's look at some defining elements from Proverbs.

"Strength and honor are her clothing" (Proverbs 31:25 NKJV).

Hebrew: *Strength*—security, majesty, power, strong [fortified against stumbling or ensnaring].

Honor—to favor, beautify, ornament, comeliness [pleasant to look at].

Mamma D, my mother-in-law and one of the lovliest women I know, is still dressing up to look fabulous and still loves to shop. Just a few weeks ago in Norfolk, England, we went on a little tour of exceptional second-hand boutiques that this area is famous for. We spotted a gorgeous white fine-ribbed sweater. I tried it on, and her response—referring to Steve, her son—was, "He's going to love you in that."

Now don't you think that's just the sweetest at ninety-three years old? She certainly hasn't lost any of her insight. When she was eighty-seven, I asked her to comment on how women dress. She said, "Most women dress for everyone else except their husbands, and at home they look like rag-bags. It doesn't make too much sense."

Will we be willing to make those small adjustments? Are we prepared to see that we may have gotten off-track and become careless in the way we dress? The cement that holds the bricks together in the construction of a building is not the biggest part, but it is absolutely essential to the cohesion of the whole. Let us beware of crumbling areas. There are things in marriage that we do not have control over, but dressing well, even on a limited budget, is a wonderful feeling personally and will only serve to enhance your marriage.

Accepting ourselves, knowing our inestimable worth, and being at ease in our own skin can be something we experience continually. It can begin with gratitude to God for painstakingly forming our parts and knitting us together. (See Psalm 139:13.) He will enable us to discover who we really are and has given us a loveliness that is unique. We, individually, are the only ones who can carry it.

So what should I do if my husband doesn't care about how I look or what I wear? When the Lord is teaching and drawing my attention to something He wants to change in me, it has been my experience that

He is neither pushy nor "in my face." In fact, I think that I could use the words *woo* and *invite*.

Perhaps there is a clue for us here. If my husband hasn't noticed me or complimented me for a long time, could it be that he needs some imaginative nudging? This might seem a bit risky, in case he is still not going to liven up at seeing you. Start in the bedroom. Plan to create an atmosphere and wear something special to catch his eye. Let me say here that there are times when he will be so preoccupied with concerns and anxieties that it will be almost impossible for him to notice.

Don't give up in this area. We crave to be noticed and so do our husbands. This is one of God's gifts. The Amplified Bible puts "notice him" along with the other parts of respect. Let it be a secret plan between you and the Lord to waken your beloved to you. Don't forget to pray about it. Sooner or later, at the most unexpected time, he will notice you and let you know. Besides, when we make those efforts, we end up having fun and feeling good about ourselves.

Not to confuse you, but we do need to remember that maintaining the health of our inner woman is more important than any number of externals. One morning, curled up on our sofa, wearing a bathrobe and no makeup and my hair awry, Steve said, right out of the blue, "Trishie, you're so beautiful." Knock your socks off! What did he see?

All I could come up with was that I was both at peace and cheerful. Cheerful is huge! Ask the Holy Spirit of God to ignite your imagination. You and your husband are unique—no one else is like either of you. This is why each marriage has its own dynamic.

At the other end of the spectrum, there can be an unhealthy fixation on dress and appearance. Advertisements, commercials, shop windows, etc., all have their own power to draw us into a certain compulsion with what is the current fashion. There is a balance between not caring how we look and being obsessed with externals. You don't have to be wearing the very latest design to look wonderful. In fact, find your own style and grow in it.

Be careful of competition—it is always unsatisfactory. At every level there will inevitably be somebody with more beauty, more money, more square feet, more horsepower, more degrees, and more to say. For the Christian, Christ is the center, not me. This is the secret of contentment.

Let's be beautiful from the inside out. Inner beauty, with its various attributes, is meticulously cultivated over many years. This is our substance, our solid worth, our actual possession. Outer beauty is the presentation of that substance. Think of it as the frame around the picture.

CHAPTER 17

MODESTY: A MAGNETISM
ALL ITS OWN

"Let not your adornment be merely external."
—1 Peter 3:4
"Women should adorn themselves modestly"
—1 Timothy 2:9–10

THESE SCRIPTURES SERVE as signposts in our desire to find the equilibrium between beauty and modesty. The Bible has a timeless relevance. We tend to swing to extremes, but the Bible calls us to a wonderful balance of wholeness and delight.

Greek: *Modest*—orderly, i.e., decorous of good behavior.

Does the way we dress evoke good behavior in us and in others?

Oxford Dictionary: *Modesty*—not violating good taste, not violating propriety, dignified, decent, scrupulously chaste, not excessive of things, unpretentious in appearance, correctness of behavior or morals.

"You are not your own. You were bought with a price [purchased with a preciousness and paid for, made His own.] So then honor God and bring glory to Him in your body" (1 Corinthians 6:20).

What is modesty anyway? I know we are not supposed to notice, but the current trend in our local churches is to show as much cleavage as possible. Because many churches have theatre seats, greeting time can be quite a challenge for the men. The conscientious don't know where to look. The safest is for them to look the women in the eye, even if it means getting a stiff neck.

Last week we were enjoying a delicious meal with a wonderful couple. We were just up a hill from the ocean with several islands out beyond us. It was such a great place to eat.

Our waitress was friendly and helpful, smartly turned out and amply endowed. Whenever she leaned over to care for us, everything she had tumbled out across the table! She may well have been embarrassed if she had checked herself in the mirror beforehand. Then again, maybe not. Somehow it isn't a surprise in a restaurant, but it's a disgrace in church. I think there are times when our grandmothers would be ashamed of us.

Dannah Gresh, author of that excellent book *And the Bride Wore White* wrote in *Today's Christian Woman,* "The truth is Christian men struggle deeply with visual temptation and mental sexual sin. Ask more than half the men who attended a recent Promise Keepers conference and admitted to viewing pornography the week preceding the event. Ask the pastors, struggling with online porn, who regularly call Focus on the Family's pastoral care line. Recently the men Bob ministers to have admitted that there's a new place where temptation is a problem. "I'm struggling with the way women dress in church," they confess. It's the placement of the temptation that makes them feel so vulnerable.

One last point to highlight: "Immodesty isn't just about causing our Christian brothers to stumble; it's about craving for the emotional rush we receive when we know we are being noticed." Thank you for your honesty and vulnerability, Dannah.

I clearly admit the struggle with current fashion trends. I was delighted when there was a distinct shift from the shapeless dull racks of women's clothing to a feminine flair with belts and jackets accenting our waistlines and flowing skirts and blouses with the odd frill. Yet along with this welcome change came the classy blouses where the top button had definitely dropped two buttons from previous styles and the necklines were on the plunge. Admittedly, there is something very attractive about an open neck, but there is a line, and when we cross it, we know. And so do the men in our company.

In my own search for what is acceptable, I often ask Steve, and he always tries to give me an honest appraisal. Another way to reach the core of our intentions is to stand in front of the mirror and say, "Lord, how do I look? Can I go out dressed like this and represent you?" Then, when shopping, ask Him about a garment that catches your eye: "Does this fit in the wardrobe of a princess belonging to another king, to another kingdom?"

"Should your fountains be dispersed abroad, streams of water in the streets? Let them be only your own, and not for strangers with you" (Proverbs 5:16–17 NKJV).

Being publicly provocative in our dress is carelessly letting our gifted source of refreshment be available to lustful and hungry eyes. Worse yet, we undoubtedly cause the unwary to stumble and many of them fall. Maybe girls and women who dress in this way should carry a little sign in front of them, saying, "Careful, floor slippery!" The sign would be embarrassing. Admittedly there are tremendous pressures from the world and from our peers.

The nobility on our heads, as daughters of the King, is beyond any earth-bound majesty. What do we gain skirting the edges of seduction? If we listen carefully, we will hear a distant call to set a standard that would please the Lord. I promise you, the rewards of turning the biblical key of modesty on our closet doors will bring the oil of joy upon our heads. There will come a quality to our lives that will be undeniable and unduplicated. I wonder if we have ever truly grasped how much magnetism comes with delicate modesty.

CHAPTER 18

WONDERFUL BEDROOMS FOR GLORIOUS SEX

H OW DO YOU feel about your bedroom? How does your husband feel when he walks into the most intimate room of your marriage?

"She makes herself coverings of tapestry" (Proverbs 31:22).

Hebrew: *Coverings*—coverlet, to spread, to deck.

Oxford: *To deck*—to adorn.

To adorn—to add beauty or luster, to furnish with ornaments.

This describes her bed. I hope this is already giving us ideas! Some will be surprised that scripture is explicit and detailed in matters relating to the marriage bed and the bedding. We observe in Proverbs 31 that the lady of virtue described applied herself with effort to create beauty and orderliness. What have you taken time to create?

Sexual Union Is Good and Right and Proper

It expresses the deepest, most exclusive intimacy and the most explosive creativity. Let there be love, respect, and laughter, but also gentleness and abandoned freedom with each other. "Therefore, a man shall leave his father and his mother and shall become united and cleave to his wife, and they shall become one flesh" (Genesis 2:24).

The Bedroom and the Marriage Bed Are a Place of Comfort

"And Isaac brought her into his mother, Sarah's, tent, and he took Rebekah, and she became his wife, and he loved her. Thus Isaac was comforted after his mother's death" (Genesis 24:67).

The Bedroom Is for Relaxation and Play

Read the delightful passages from Song of Songs 2:8–17 and Song of Songs 4:1–16 for inspiration, and enjoy the exquisite wonder of pure romance.

The First Year Is Set Apart

"When a man is newly married, he shall not go out with the army or be charged with any business: he shall be free at home one year, and shall cheer his wife whom he has taken" (Deuteronomy 24:5 NIV).

Hebrew: *Cheer*—delight in, make very glad, make her merry and joyful.

Fruit and Flowers

Steve buys flowers for me, so one day many years ago I had the idea of going to a florist to have a masculine bouquet created for him. I left the arrangement with a little card on his bedside table where he couldn't miss it.

"Is this for me? Thank you, Trishie, thank you!" His response was overwhelming. Another possibility is a small bowl of fresh fruit. It is always a welcome sight and shows you made an effort to please and surprise him.

Fragrance

Keep your bed linen fresh and fragrant. Dry your sheets outside when you can. The breezes fill them with the distant perfume of a thousand flowers in the spring and summer. These little details are worth the effort.

"The fragrance of your garments is like the fragrance of Lebanon" (Song of Songs 4:11).

Fresh, fresh, be and keep fresh!

Storage

Please don't allow your bedroom to become a "dump-all," but let it be loaded with a certain eloquence and welcome. Find another space for the magazines, the towels, the telephone notes, and the laundry.

Television

You may want to seriously consider bucking the recent trend to share the bedroom with CNN, Larry, Oprah, the Dolphins and the Redskins. They seem to have gained admission to that private, honorable, and superlative room called the master bedroom. It is supposed to be the perfect place for those intimate and private conversations that you need to have together.

"You know darling, we have those nice reclining chairs for when we watch the game; let's keep the bedroom just for us!"

Decorate

Do not be afraid to spend on your bedroom. Forgo a few little extras and soon you'll have enough to make an amazing difference for your husband and for you. Fresh paint is not expensive. Involve the Lord—God is interested and would love to be included.

Create Carefully Planned Pleasures for Your Husband

"The mandrakes give off a fragrance; at our gates are pleasant fruits; all manner new and old which I have laid up for you, my beloved" (Song of Songs 7:13).

Now, what about us? You can have a designer bedroom and be an absolute bear to go to bed with. When was the last time you put on something sweet and spicy, downright gorgeous, exclusively for your bedroom? Do your husband a favor and don't always wear his comfortable boxers to bed. Throw out those faded, dull, and uninteresting items. Why should your man come home to a wife in the same old, same old. Remember those honeymoon preparations you made months before your wedding date?

Jewelry

So what does the ancient book of the Song of Songs tell us? Simply that jewelry has the potential of ravishing a man's heart. On occasion, why not wear jewelry to bed? "You have ravished my heart with one look of your eyes, with one link of your necklace" (Song of Songs 4:9 NKJV).

Our bedrooms, tiny or large, simply furnished or lavish, are to be a sanctuary. They should be our refuge, our port in a storm, our hideaway of safety, our oasis to preserve intimacy, our carefully prepared sanctum.

CHAPTER 19

TWO SPLENDID PILLARS

IN THE ENHANCEMENT of our womanhood, what is it that God Himself finds both precious and expensive? Imagine yourself in this scene:

> They both stepped out of the Bentley, red stitching on parchment leather seats. Footmen held open the doors, and she took his arm as they headed inside. She was simply splendid, tall and regal, with a long silk gown and immaculate hairstyle. He, with bold tie and a striped shirt finished with a black blazer and brass buttons, strode purposefully beside her. As they entered the banquet hall all eyes turned in their direction. There was a lowering of voices as little groups commented discretely on their arrival. At the table, all was elegance and style with fine china, crystal, flowers, and gilt-edged nametags. He held her chair as she sat, jewelry glinting in the halogen lights.

> What a proud man he must be, you thought, with such an exquisitely elegant lady for his wife. It was not so. The conversation flowed easily at first, places they had visited, unusual happenings, interesting people, but a strange phenomenon began to surface. Everything he said or commented on was apparently inaccurate. At one point there were

six consecutive sentences that she corrected, or at least adjusted. It became apparent that a vital part of her being was vested in belittling him. Suddenly the glamour was gone, the beauty faded, and her inner person was on display for all to see. It was not pleasant to behold.

Mere external adornment in hair and dress and jewels will be inadequate, no matter how elaborate. A certain poverty of person will still cling to us. The scriptures encourage us to give attention to what is hidden—who we are beneath the skin. We are invited to invest extravagantly in what is described as "incorruptible," something that will not decay with use or time.

So what is to be the valuable purchase? While browsing in this high-end boutique, be looking for two extremely costly commodities. One is *meekness*, the other is *quietness*.

"But [let it be] the hidden man [woman] of the heart, in that which is not corruptible, [even the ornament] of a meek and quiet spirit, which is in the sight of God of great price" (1 Peter 3:4 KJV).

My artistic friend Jude put together a PowerPoint presentation for the taught courses, "Transforming Keys." She chose two gleaming Greek pillars to picture these qualities. Before you run for cover, let me describe each of them.

Greek: *Meek*—gentle, calm, soothing.

Oxford Dictionary: *Soothing*—calming persons, nerves, and passions; to soften pain.

The second commodity is a quiet spirit.

Greek: *Quiet*—undisturbed, undisturbing.

The Amplified Bible throws light on what this does *not* look like in the verse above—*not* anxious, *not* wrought up.

This does not mean I am to be a mouse in the house, but I confess that whenever I remember these two defining elements of a quiet spirit I am set back on my heels. Between the two of them, they cut straight through so much of my life. So easily I'm disturbed, and so quickly, I can be disturbing. Yet undisturbed and undisturbing both have a strong beckoning power. They remind me of two gentle handmaidens nudging me back onto the path where I belong. I find my heart responding with desire to walk in obedience. These two qualities, meekness and quietness, are included in the Divine choice for our jewelry.

CHAPTER 20

THE UNAFFORDABLE LUXURY

> "I was asleep but my heart was awake. A voice!
> My beloved was knocking."
> —Song of Songs 5:2 NASB

S HE WAS ASLEEP, but her heart was wakeful. Was that the voice of my beloved calling my name? Then she heard it—a soft knocking, a voice to her as familiar as her own. "Open to me, my sister, my darling, my dove, my perfect one!"

Knowing he would not enter uninvited, she waited and heard him speak of the cold, the chill outside. "My head is drenched with dew, my locks with the damp of the night."

Solomon's Song of Songs is a love song and vividly describes sexual reluctance.

Excuses mustered an army. Weary and ready for bed, how could she dress again? Her feet were washed, why dirty them? Then her beloved put his hand into the latch opening and his fingers on the handles of the bolt. Her heart was stirred for him; she got up to open the door. Her own hands now dripping with the sweet liquid myrrh he had left on the latch. She opened the door, stunned. Only the emptiness of the dark greeted her. Her beloved had disappeared. He was gone.

Quickly she dressed and threw on a large silk mantle against the elements. She ran out into the night looking, searching, calling, but no answer came. The watchmen that swept the streets of loose and immoral women caught sight of her. They hit out and wounded her, snatching away the veil and mantle. *How different it could have been*, she thought. Now she was cold and alone.

Before I begin my confession, please know I am passionately in love with my husband. We have a wonderful marriage and after thirty-seven years are closer and more in love than ever. We have known both storms and drought and have seen abundant harvests. We have walked the years together in a broken world.

I call it the thick drape that is sometimes drawn between us. It is almost imperceptible. Ladies, you know as well as I do that our amazing men have intense powers to focus on one thing at a time. As for us, we have the astonishing capacity to listen to two conversations at once while we plan what we will serve for supper. When my husband drops a hint about making love, and I'm not in the mood, I shift the point of interest to jet engines or the price of fuel, and he's away. All the while he's not totally unaware, and if I continue my little games even to the bedroom, by now he's truly got the message. He tumbles into bed and, with a kind goodnight, is soundly asleep in minutes. Meanwhile, I, the oh-so-tired Trish, am now wide awake. Sleep has fled away, and I feel the brush of that closed thick drape.

You may find this hard to believe, but I've come to realize, and biblically so, that Satan has cunning and wily designs to draw us into disobedient and lonely pathways. Tell me, please, how is it that when we were courting and keeping a standard of purity before marriage, we were dying to go to bed together? Now, when the world of marriage is spread out before us like a country to be explored, we women periodically experience reluctance? You may well disagree with me, but I believe the devil himself has a hand in it. Why? This is one of the most significant and deepest dimensions of marriage. If he can, he will cause dysfunction in this area. Then he will have gained and stolen precious territory.

Believe me, I have heard from bleeding hearts of much attending pain in the area of the marriage bed; pain from infidelity and cheating spouses; pain from sordid pasts; pain from the invasion of pornography; and sometimes pain from downright ignorance.

Another major issue is the overcommitted lives we live today. Women may become completely disinterested in sexual togetherness with their husbands because they have worn themselves out. It is easy to be overstressed, or just plain depleted, for one reason or another. Long term, this can become a significant problem in marriage. It would be so good to work together on priorities and perhaps some simplification.

We have now the greatest possible news for those who know and follow Jesus. According to the ancient prophet, what has been eaten, chewed, and stripped away—even for years—can actually be restored by the power of a loving and compassionate God.

> Then I will make up to you for the years that the swarming locust has eaten, the creeping locust, the stripping locust, and the gnawing locust. My great army which I sent among you. And you shall have plenty to eat and be satisfied, and praise the name of the Lord your God. And there is no other, and my people will never be put to shame.
> —Joel 2:25–26 NASB

In my own journey of periodic moody reticence, and in my study of scripture, I came to see that I needed at such times to change direction. I've come to call it "the unaffordable luxury." The highest reason to be available is the personal intimacy in marriage. However, the wise among us are also quietly aware that there are opposing forces continuously attempting to stimulate and entice our husbands in people, in magazines, advertisements, and on the Internet. There is a veritable avalanche of seduction and defilement present in the western world. Only the diligent will apply themselves successfully to overcome it, and they will receive the consequent rewards.

Shauntie Feldman, in her brilliant book, *For Women Only*, writes of a man's deep emotional need to be wanted. She says that sex is more than a physical need. When it is missing, it is as emotionally serious to him as, say, his sudden silence would be to you were he to simply stop communicating with you. It is just as wounding to him, just as much a legitimate grievance, and just as dangerous to your marriage.

Hear what Paul the apostle says about it:

> Is it good to have sexual relations? Certainly, but only within a certain context. It is good for a man to have a wife, and for a woman to have a husband. Sexual drives are strong, but marriage is strong enough to contain them, and to provide for a balanced and fulfilling sexual life in a world of sexual disorder. The marriage bed must be a place of mutuality, the husband seeking to satisfy his wife, and the wife seeking to satisfy her husband. Marriage is not a place to stand up for your rights. Marriage is a decision to serve the other, whether in bed or not. Abstaining from sex is permissible for a period of time if you both agree to it, and if it's for the purpose of prayer and fasting—but only for such time. Then come back together again. Satan has an ingenious way of tempting us when we least expect it. I'm not, understand, commanding these periods of abstinence, only providing my best council if you should choose them.
>
> —1 Corinthians 7:1–6 TM

Let's look especially at verse 5 in the Amplified version: "Do not refuse and deprive and defraud each other [of your due marital rights], except perhaps by mutual consent for a time, so that you may devote yourself unhindered to prayer" (1 Corinthians 7:5).

Greek: *To defraud*—to deprive, to despoil.
Oxford Dictionary: *To despoil*—to plunder, to rob.

This particular passage in its clear instruction, along with our response of obedience, is a bastion and fortress against infidelity.

"Marriage should be honored by all, and the marriage bed kept pure, for God will judge the adulterer and all the sexually immoral" (Hebrews 13:4 NIV).

Greek: *Honored*—valuable, costly, esteemed of highest degree, beloved, more and most precious (all superlatives).

Our bedrooms and our marriage beds are treasure troves where life's costliest perfume is poured out. Why would we be duped into indulging ourselves in the unaffordable luxury of withholding the power of our bodies from our husbands?

CHAPTER 21

THE PATH TO CONCEALMENT
AND BETRAYAL

IN THIS CHAPTER I want to address the boundaries of the heart, particularly for us women. Shall I begin to count on my fingers the men we know who have been betrayed by their wives and cheated out of life's most intimate relationship by concealed affairs? Then what of the women whose hearts are left ripped and bleeding by best friends who have stolen away their husbands?

My husband's striking cousin told of a friend and confidant who ate at her table and enjoyed all those privileges best friends do. Laurel and her husband were a picture-perfect family, with five fine children and Daddy looking for promotion in his company. Obviously, in all these situations both parties share some blame, but suddenly and with no warning, her husband, the love of her life, was stolen away forever.

To be betrayed by one you trust and love is a deep wound many marriages and families suffer. The first, most telling sign of a fracturing relationship is concealment. It was so between God and Adam in the garden of Eden, and it is so throughout human history. The closer and more intimate the relationship, the deeper the pain of betrayal. There are numerous references to betrayal in the New Testament. Most of them refer to Judas Iscariot, disciple and follower of Jesus. In all cases the Greek word *paradidomi* is the same.

Greek: *Betrayal*—to surrender, i.e., yield up, entrust, transmit.

I find this incredibly enlightening as to what happens when some form of betrayal takes place. Someone has surrendered something. Someone has yielded up something. Someone has entrusted to someone else what should not have been entrusted to that person.

Rhonda was thirty-five, feeling and looking great. She had been and still was a very busy mom. A successful husband had provided amply for their smooth, unruffled lifestyle. They were very much in love. He was extremely busy and upwardly mobile.

A luncheon date with a girlfriend hadn't panned out, so she was at a bit of a loose end and bored, though she'd never admit it. She casually dropped into the public library to browse.

"Why, Rhonda! How great to see you!" She was totally surprised to find a friend she hadn't seen since college days. He was tall, tanned, and sandy-haired. He wore an open checked shirt and a doeskin jacket, along with that unmistakable air of wealth and confidence. After the enthusiastic greetings, she didn't miss his comment about how good she looked and that she hadn't changed a bit.

"Let's go for coffee," he invited.

It had been several days now since her husband had noticed her. What else was there to do? She had a full hour before an afternoon appointment. Mind you, a red flag did go up in her mind over coffee as he began to pour out his sad story of a broken marriage relationship.

While preparing evening dinner, she found her thoughts preoccupied. She even felt a little rush as she reflected on the attentions of her college friend. When her husband breezed in, bright and happy and full of the news of his day, she found herself wishing he would notice that she had dressed especially for dinner. Slowly, she realized that some boundary of the heart had been crossed, and yes, that red flag was flapping away in the winds of her spirit. Suddenly she knew what she must do.

Early in their marriage she and her husband Britch had established for themselves the safety net of mutual accountability. She must tell him everything that had happened at the library and over coffee. Full of reluctance, she flashed up a quick prayer and blurted out the whole episode.

Britch's response surprised her. It was as though her transparency woke him from a long stupor. He gathered her into his strong arms and suddenly really looked at her. Relief coursed through her body as they settled into the quietude and safety of their own home for the evening.

Sadly, not every story with parallel happenings ends like this. Crossing the God-given boundaries of the heart can turn perilous, quickly exposing us to future danger. Tragically, it plunges marriages and children into gut-wrenching anguish. The results are always attended with the ugly immediate as well as the crushing long-term consequences that come from teaming up with the devil. This is why we are called to guard our hearts. "Watch over your heart with all diligence, for from it [flow] the springs of life" (Proverbs 4:23).

Above all, my heart is to be guarded. More to the point, I am to be occupied in guarding it. The defining Hebrew word *springs* is "boundaries." We deeply know that boundaries are set for our protection and safety. These lines are not casual but essential. They're not enough in themselves; they need guarding against marauding forces of all shapes and sizes. Some are sophisticated and others more obviously dangerous. There is a finely engineered plot afoot in the world to destroy marriages and families. This multi-faceted scheme, organized from the dark side, sets up many magnetic traps. Some of these have the appearance of innocence at first and intrigue our curiosity. If we are not alert to them we are easily lured into compromise.

Among many deceitful snares that can undermine our commitment to fidelity, watch out for:

- A flirtation in a chat room
- Responding to an uninvited, inappropriate e-mail
- The magazine you hide when company's coming
- The channel you change when someone unexpectedly enters the room
- The illegitimate rendezvous that you keep as a thrilling secret
- The unrestrained notice of some attractive other, particularly when coupled with later imaginations
- Internet surfing in the small hours of the morning that no one knows about

We need a strategy, a plan, a predetermination. The prophet Daniel determined in his heart that he would not defile himself. (See Daniel 1:8.) He lived in exile in the sumptuous court of four successive Babylonian kings. Nobody in the king's cabinet would have known or cared if he compromised the character of his God. He proved this purpose of his heart to be true throughout his life, although his steadfastness was often assailed.

I was so struck a while ago with the fact that the streets of the heavenly city being prepared for us by Christ are built of pure, transparent gold. It is apparent if we think about it that nothing can be hidden there! How great to clear away all concealments and hidings before our time comes to reside in that amazing place.

What about you? What is your situation? Did you come home from shopping for groceries and find a note with a scrawled message on the kitchen table—your husband mustering inelegant prose to advise you he would not be coming back, ever? For some, such a statement comes unexpectedly, right out of the blue. For some, it only confirms a protracted, gnawing uneasiness.

Has such a blinding, colossal revelation ripped through your life, leaving you stunned and angry? Where can you turn at such a time? People in your life, both near and far, will seem to take sides. Some will be full of sympathy and support for you as you navigate your little boat down this life-threatening waterfall. Others will distance themselves. Even previously close friends will find you, now a single, a threat to their own marriages.

Invariably, the spouse is emotionally, as well as physically, trapped in an affair. The brute strength of the cords which tie to this immoral alliance is too much for both of you. What can you do? Here are a few lines of a poem you will find in the chapter on forgiveness, which may help you to take the step of dropping to your knees and pouring the whole mess out to God.

> There is a cross where you may go
> To pour it out, your tale of woe.
> A place so safe, you need not hold
> It back, a single word, be bold.

If anyone's heart bleeds and hurts for you, the Lord's does. Isaiah prophesied, "Surely, He has born our griefs (sicknesses, weaknesses, and distresses) and carried our sorrows and pains" (Isaiah 53:4).

In spite of the thunderous messages of hopelessness that pound against the walls of your mind, the scriptures will bring you hope from God Himself.

I remember attending an intimate house wedding where an exquisite bride in ivory and a strong attractive groom in black joined hands before their pastor and close friends to renew their wedding vows. Their marriage had been totally demolished by concealment and betrayal. Sometimes—sometimes— "Powers of love can turn from hate, and hope swing wide the longed for gate." ("Virtues Path" Chapter 7)

Our hearts go out to the ladies out there who have suffered dreadfully at the hands of their husbands and who live with deep sorrows. In such a fallen world, and in the modern age, there have been unspeakable examples of Prince Charming turning into a monster. If this speaks to you, may you have wisdom from the presence of the Lord, and may you find deep solace in the Psalms.

It is inconceivable to me that a man would beat his wife and physically attack her, but it does happen. You conceal your bruises and put on the bravest face you can muster. You keep going for the children, for the family, for the church, or simply because you don't know what else to do. You are tied to this man financially and emotionally, and you don't know where to turn. I feel such sorrow when I consider that our churches have so failed you.

In many instances, where you should have received help and refuge, you have been blindsided with spiritual platitudes. "It will be all right, dearie, we will pray for you. I'm sure it won't recur." You are equally sure that it will! No one has had courage enough to face off with this brutal man who struts about, often with a veneer of outward spirituality. What a horrendous tension you have lived with. You long to be a good wife, but all the elasticity has gone from your heart.

There is no good reason to think that your situation will improve. If the abuse continues periodically, it would be wise to obtain outside support and a secret refuge with whatever financial means can be secured. The money issues should not dictate the misery issues. Our gracious Shepherd will care for the practical needs. God does not expect you or your children to continue in such a situation.

Our own limited experience is that the physical removal of the abused was the only step—and the first step—toward establishing reality in the mind of the abuser. He will usually experience considerable shock, and substantial time should elapse for this to make a sufficient impression. Your move could possibly be the beginning of the long road toward normalcy. May God graciously raise up a wider availability of stable hearts and homes to offer both wise care and shelter for your situation.

CHAPTER 22

HER HUSBAND BOASTS

H AVE YOU EVER measured a man's rib or even weighed it? In our wildest moments, and in our most heady brilliance, let's remember that that's what God started with.

> So the Lord God caused the man to fall into a deep sleep and while he was sleeping He took one of the man's ribs and closed up the place with flesh. Then the Lord God made a woman from the rib he had taken out of the man. And he brought her to the man, the man said, "This is now bone of my bones and flesh of my flesh. She shall be called woman."
>
> —Genesis 2:21

"Her husband is known in the gate" (Proverbs 21:23).

A great story is told of a man who was a keynote speaker at a Promise Keepers rally. After he addressed a packed crowd of men, his message was so impacting that all 30,000 stood to their feet and gave him an ovation. Women don't attend Promise Keepers, but there was one woman there that day. She was under the platform waiting for her husband. She heard the roar of the crowd and the stamp of feet. When he finally disappeared backstage and went downstairs, this is what she said, "I don't know what you told them, but I know you live every word." Do you know what he said in reply? He said that her words of affirmation meant more to him than the standing ovation of all those men.

"A virtuous woman is a crown to her husband" (Proverbs 12:4).

Always remember that ours is the power to crown our husbands, to honor their headship under Christ. God has so ordained it that ours is the tribute and the cheering they crave.

Hebrew: *Crown*—to encircle for protection, especially to crown literally or figuratively.

Note also that wisdom is personified in the feminine, as a lady crowning the man!

> Wisdom is supreme, therefore get wisdom. Though it cost all you have, get understanding. Esteem her and she will exalt you, embrace her, and she will honor you. She will set a garland of grace on your head and present you with a crown of splendor.
>
> —Proverbs 4:7–9

The woman of worth (virtue) in Proverbs 31 does not hinder or block her husband's leadership; she makes way for it. She enjoys a mate with leadership qualifications. How does this happen, even if she's convinced of her own opinion?

> She consults him.
> She refers to him.
> She defers to him.
> She talks it out with him.

I asked Mamma D, now a widow of eight years, what she missed most about Papa. "I miss talking things over with him," she said.

As for me, I get worked up over a problem, stew, and get anxious. I can't see a solution or exit. Then I ask myself, *Why don't I ask Steve?* I do, and—sometimes—poof, the light comes on!

As to our husbands' headship relating to the children, if we always answer all their questions and solve all their problems, we will soon be well-established as the primary parent. Our husbands will graciously see what a "good job" we're doing and will slowly abdicate. If we understood how our husbands tick, we would be wise to steer the children as often as possible to their daddy, determining to provide a united front for them, and supporting him fully. The only exception, of course, would be a violation of God's moral law.

This deference to him relating to the children will ease your load massively and will increase his sense of responsibility. He will grow and develop in leadership and headship. I hear women say, "I wish my husband was a spiritual leader," yet they have never moved aside to give him the role he was created to fulfill.

"Now I want you to realize that the head of every man is Christ [any objections at this point?] and the head of the woman is the man" (2 Corinthians 11:3).

Your husband's headship in marriage is an authority and position appointed by God Himself. Please make a mental note that this *is* a fact—present tense! Surprisingly, his growth and success here are things you have a lot to do with.

Consider making intentional, deliberate room for his leadership and his headship. If you struggle in this area, it helps to recognize that subduing ourselves to our husband's leadership is the supreme expression of our independence. Why is this an independent choice? Because we retain to ourselves the option to submit or not.

"But the woman is the glory of man" (1 Corinthians 11:7 NKJV).

Greek: *Glory*—dignity, honor, praise, from the base of a word that means pleasure.

"Darling, did you know that I'm supposed to be your glory, your dignity, honor, and praise?"

Tell me, why do we allow ourselves to be stirred up to contesting, to ruling, to bossiness, and to rudely pushing ourselves ahead of our husbands? Why do we grasp at independence and self-actualization when our true calling comes to us on the gentle wings of a dove, on the strong wings of an eagle, by the gracious Holy Spirit? The deep, delicious unfolding of the mystery is that we lose our life in order to find it.

"If you cling to your life, you will lose it; but if you give it up for Me, you will find it" (Matthew 10:39 NLT).

"Her children rise up and call her blessed, her husband also, and he praises her" (Proverbs 31:28).

Her reward is a proud and happy husband. Here we have a husband whose enthusiasm for his wife is irrepressible, and it shows. If you feel uncelebrated, and he never raves about you, ask yourself why. You could ask him, or better still, be mysteriously feminine and try one of the keys we have been discussing.

Hebrew: *Praise*—to shine, to make a show, to boast, to be clamorously foolish, to rave, to celebrate, to feign itself madness (as in "He is madly in love with her").

Now it's my turn to notice and prefer my husband. One of life's greatest pleasures is to keep my eyes for Steve and to notice and admire him every day. When he first stepped, or rather rocketed, into my life, I noticed two things: his intense, well-shaped eyes and his soccer knees. Now, after thirty-seven years, there is so much that I adore. He always lights up when I express admiration for his character and his body, and when I put words to my gratitude for all that he does for me and the laughter he brings.

> However, let each man of you (without exception) love his wife as [being in a sense] his very own self; and let the wife see that she respects and reverences her husband—that she notices him, regards him, honors him, prefers him, venerates and esteems him; and that she defers to him, praises him, and loves and admires him exceedingly.
> —Ephesians 5:33

Oxford: *Defers*—courteous regard, hold in deep unusual affection, make concessions, respect.

Let's camp momentarily on *defers* as to making concessions. Please don't expect your beloved to think and do things the way you do. We are detailed, they are comprehensive. So when he helps you with the dishes or the kitchen after a meal, thank him heartily and don't tell him he's misplacing things or not doing it right. Really, it's so belittling to correct a man when he's willing to help you.

Don't ever correct your husband in public. Sometimes it may mean biting your tongue half off, but if you demean him, your gains will be meager, if any, and your losses difficult to recoup.

"As the church is subject to Christ, so let wives also be subject in everything to their husbands" (Ephesians 5:24).

As women of the twenty-first century, if there was ever a place in our reading of scripture that we would wonder about the translation, it would be in verse 24. *Everything*, Lord?

I do pray that as we have journeyed together this far, you have come to see that submission is not a bad word but a door to major freedoms and fulfillment for us as women. The truth of submission, so hammered and even despised, is like a well-cut, flawless diamond catching the light of the sun and throwing brilliant colors around the room. We will find it is a canopy of protection if we choose to be obedient.

On one hand, I view my husband in awe and deep affection and respect. Yet this very man, when in jeopardy or under pressure, runs to me for refuge. His favor is like the sunrise. This makes even a tiny cloud between us as black as a threatening thunderstorm in comparison.

In conclusion, to fall patiently into step with Jesus, on the biblical path outlined for us, will eventually draw from our husbands the momentous attributes we crave. As this happens over time, it will make us feel like a queen married to the most wonderful guy in the world. In a submissive and graceful dance with our husbands, we represent Christ and His church. On the open stage of the universe we are observed by beings, both good and evil, showing by our example how wise God is! You can study this in Ephesians chapters three and five.

I have only included these things because for some of you it will so hugely upgrade the remaining years that the Lord gives. The challenge is terrific. Only Christ enables it in our lives. The reasons are bound up in eternity. The rewards are beyond what we could ask or dream of. Have you been missing this key on your key ring? Try it; you can turn it in the lock to your husband's heart.

CHAPTER 23

KEYS TO YOUR CHILD'S HEART

"Your sons, whom you will make princes in all the land."
—Psalm 45:16

IN PROVERBS 31, Lemuel, king of Massa, reflects back on the days when his mother took him aside with love and firmness and taught him. It is as if she took her son by the shoulders and verbally shook him to warn him against wantonness.

Did you know that God has conferred on you as a mother a call and command to instruct your children as to truth and wisdom? We must tend to this command with diligence, with tenacity, and with passion. We cannot afford to leave this essential part of our children's journey to others when we are clearly commanded to care for it ourselves.

In Scotland, children were sent off to school with "brose and Proverbs." Brose is hot water poured over uncooked oatmeal and, with that as breakfast, the godly parents also instructed their offspring from the book of Proverbs.

You shall whet and sharpen them so as to make them penetrate, and teach and impress them diligently upon the [minds and] hearts of your

children, and shall talk of them when you sit in your house and when
you walk by the way, and when you lie down and when you rise up.
—Deuteronomy 6:7

Lemuel's mother remembers who this boy is. He came from her own
womb! Before his birth he was a son of vows made. She had transacted
with God before he was conceived. Here she establishes something that
unequivocally belongs to her, her right to teach her son. Now she begins
to unburden her mother's heart, so full of warning and insight.

Can you hear her words coming from the depth of who she is? "Oh,
my son, oh, son of my womb, oh, son of my vows." (Repetition in the
Hebrew language is for emphasis.) She teaches under the authority of
God's command. She teaches the "son of her own womb," for whom
she passed the gates of death to give life.

This young prince is not a happenstance. No child is. He comes
from the anguish of vows and promises. She has done business with the
Almighty over this handsome young man. Will she let him slip into the
all-too-ready clutches of youthful lusts? No way!

Susanna Wesley, mother of John and Charles Wesley, British
evangelists of the nineteenth century, had nineteen children. Only ten of
them survived. For each remaining child she allocated one hour per week
for spiritual instruction. Susanna is known to have worn a large apron.
When her many children were getting the best of her, she would sweep
the apron over her head. The children knew she had created for herself
a sanctuary to call on the Lord in prayer from under her apron.

Mentor your children! They need individual and regular time. Date
your children. Out with Mom; out with Pa; their favorite food. So what if
it's always burgers and fries! You are building bridges of communication.
You are creating a legacy that will pay generously through the years, first
to them, and then to you as well. Think about it. Should you live to
eighty years, you'll most likely have your children under your roof for
only a quarter of your lifetime.

How swiftly the days and years fly. The nest then becomes too small, and they must expand their own wings and fly away. If you have carefully and prayerfully invested in these precious minds and spirits, you will eat the fruit of your efforts for the rest of your life. Family traditions, life rhythms, hiking and camping trips, snacking together, and story times, all form the building blocks. You might like to ask mature spiritual women in your family or church to give you one or two of their own workable keys in parenting their children.

There is a sweet story I cannot pass by. My husband is from a wonderful family of six children—two boys and four girls. Rachel is tucked in the middle. Remembering the busy household that was her childhood home, she related to me a favorite and cherished memory. When they were bathed, and whenever her lovely curly hair was washed, Mamma D would hold her head on her lap and dry Rachel's hair by the fire. "It was just me and Mamma. It was my time." Do we have any idea how significantly some of the simplest gestures of life reach to nourish those we love?

Jonathan Goforth, a distinguished missionary statesman who poured out the major part of his life in inland China, writes, "My mother was careful in the early years to teach us the scriptures and to pray with us. One thing I look back to as a great blessing in my later life was Mother's habit of getting me to read the Psalms to her. I was only five years of age when I began this, but could read easily. From reading the Psalms aloud came the desire to memorize the scripture, which I continued to do with great profit."

"She watches over the affairs [the ways] of her household" (Proverbs 31:27 NIV).

Hebrew: *Watch*—to lean forward, to peer into the distance, to observe, to keep watch.

Ways—a procession, movements, comings and goings.

"Teach the young women to . . . love their children, to be discreet, chaste, keepers at home, good, obedient to their own husbands, that the word of God be not blasphemed" (Titus 2:5 KJV).

Greek: *Keeper*—a guard, beware, etc.

There is a great fact—little known—about the ancient sentry. Dreadful punishment was meted out to any who failed in his guard duty through the night. The sentry, as he stood listening and watching, held his long spear, or later his rifle with the bayonet fixed, under his chin. Why? You guessed it. Dozing off could prove perilous, even treasonous. If, in fact, it did happen, it was not for too long. Many a soldier returned from the various campaigns with leathery scars under his chin.

We women, like sentries, have a grave responsibility to know what is going on in our households and our families. In fact, I do believe that God has gifted us as wives and mothers with what some term a sixth sense that neither our children nor our husbands can conceive of.

Did you know that if you instruct your children in biblical truth in a digestible way for their young inquiring minds, you will discover that they will distinguish between what is good and what is evil? As their spirits are nourished and made strong by the truth, they will develop their own pointed discernment. Our own two children were in a place that was potentially dangerous to them spiritually. This was a childcare situation where they were invited to participate in something occult. Both encouraged the other, "Don't do it! Don't do it." Having been instructed in the scriptures, this undoubtedly was a time that they discerned with their spirits.

Beware of the occult and its posing in seemingly innocent forms. Any tampering with the dark side is highly dangerous, with its talons and claws nigh impossible to pry out!

The most vivid way I can think of personally illustrating this takes me back to a family summer vacation. We were parked by one of British Columbia's picturesque long lakes. It was breakfast time for "hungry hunters." Suddenly one of us spotted something struggling on the surface of the lake about two hundred meters from shore. It looked like an eagle, perhaps with its talons caught on something. In a flash Steve and Geoff were in the water swimming toward it. When they got there they discovered it to be a young eagle with its strength almost gone. The great bird had latched onto a fish that was too big for it to lift out of the water and the fish had headed into the deeps, taking the eagle with it. They were afraid to get too close, so they put a piece of wood under each wing, and then slowly paddled it to shore.

When it became apparent that it was no longer going to be a danger to us, we dried it in a towel and sat with it in our travel trailer, trying to keep it warm and feeding it milk and bread. Later we connected with the forest ranger, who explained what had likely happened and took charge of a few days of rehabilitation. Playing with occult things is most certainly like sinking talons into a fish that is too big.

Did you know that as parents we have a responsibility to give a clear and fully knowledgeable answer to these questions at all ages?

- Do we know where our children are and who they are with?
- Do we know what our children are thinking?
- Do we know what our children are feeling?
- Do we know what our children are watching?
- Do we know what our children are being taught?

When Billy, a first grader, bursts in from the school bus while you are fully engaged in preparing dinner, it may take everything you can muster to sit down and listen with focused attention. When Billy comes home from college, it might take the whole of the Christmas holidays before he opens his heart to you. Prayer, of course, wonderfully dissolves the hesitation!

CHAPTER 24

THE BLESSING

"Her children rise up and call her blessed."
—Proverbs 31:28

HEBREW: *BLESSED*—RIGHT, HAPPY, honest, prosperous, leading, guiding, relieving.

It would be a wholesome exercise to use the above words and bless our mothers. If it seems impossible to relate these words to your mother, remember it was she who faced off with death itself to bring you into the world. In this blessing you may find at least one word, if not all of them, to bring as a blessing to your own mother.

To My Mother:

I bless you, Mom, for you have chosen what is right for me and not what is twisted and crooked. You taught me by the way you live and the words you said that there is a reliable plumb line in the universe that begins and ends in God's heart. You chose, and still choose, what is true and honest, as opposed to what is compromising and dangerous for me, even though I might find other paths attractive.

His peace reaches deep and sure within you, despite the outside ravages against your personal world. I can taste your very happiness sometimes, when it spills over onto me. May the joy that runs full and real inside of you continue always.

I am forever grateful that you are dependable and trustworthy. I know that what you tell me is true and that I can count on you to keep my confidence. You have prospered in the deepest roots of love and affection expressed by those near and dear to you. By your example you have earned the right to lead, to instruct, to speak your mind. You are neither subtle in your suggestions nor intrusive in your manner. Believe it or not, it's hard to resist opening my very heart to you.

There are times when I am in need of guidance, to tap into the wisdom of the years. I know that if I should ask advice, you will open the windows of your own life experience, even with its accompanying vulnerabilities. I can take your words and I find them to be the language of my own story. We meet and speak as pilgrims, as eternal friends, both struggling and exulting in His purposes. You relieve me just by your presence, by the sound of your voice, by the stroking of my hair.

Mom, it has always been a comfort that you have listened without condemnation, even in painful times. You have believed in me because you believed in God for me. Thank you.

May those of us who are mothers also live to be the fulfillment of these blessings.

CHAPTER 25

THE MERRIMENT OF AGING

"She smiles at the future and laughs at old age."
—Proverbs 31:25

HEBREW: *LAUGH*—PLAY, make merry, scorn, minimize, belittle. This is the opposite of the billion-dollar cosmetics industry, which takes the aging process very seriously, frantically trying to preserve youth. I have great appreciation for the advances in scientific research that strives to preserve and recover bits and pieces of the "dew of youth" for those of us who have long since passed that lovely stage. There is also faith in some of the ancient beauty secrets that are effective and less expensive.

Nonetheless, the scripture instructs us that the sickle of old age cuts us all down in the end!

"For all men [women] are like grass, and all their glory is like the flowers of the field. The grass withers and the flowers fall, but the Word of the Lord stands for ever" (1 Peter 1:24–25).

In Ruth Graham's biography, *A Time for Remembering*, author Patricia D. Cornwell writes that as Ruth's fragile shell grew older, it seemed that the shell itself became transparent, so that more of Ruth was coming through. Her inner beauty was shining through her physical frame.

Jude, a great supporter of the "Rubies" courses passed on to me this wonderful quote from Thomas Aquinas: "The splendor of a soul in grace is so seductive that it surpasses the beauty of all created things."

"Charm is deceitful and beauty is vain" (Proverbs 31:30).

Hebrew: *Charm*—untrue, cheat, false.

Beauty—beautiful, makes itself fair, deck.

Vain—empty, transitory, unsatisfactory, from a root in Hebrew, to be vain in fact, word, or expectation, specifically to lead astray.

Without stating the obvious, be careful not to be fixated on good looks.

Flipping through an old copy of the Canadian magazine, *Chatelaine*, I came across Rona Maynard's delightful "Under the Knife."

Linda took me aside and gave me the scoop on her planned birthday gift to herself: a little work on the eyes.

"I'm sick of these bags," confided Linda, who had just turned forty-nine. "People keep telling me how tired I look."

To Linda, now energetic and vibrant after surgery, I pronounce the effect "more relaxed." As for Linda, she's delighted she looks as energetic as she feels. This year an estimated 40,000 Canadians will take the surgical route to enhance self esteem. No longer the preserve of pampered socialites, cosmetic surgery has gone mainstream.

Office workers and teachers, like Linda, are splurging on nips and tucks instead of winter vacations or new bathrooms. When a forty-plus friend calls and exclaims, "Guess what!" I wonder which body part is up for renovation ….

I know beautiful women in their seventies with faces creased like fine linen. They didn't have the option of cosmetic surgery, and they don't miss it. If they could change their bodies they would want nimbler fingers and eyes that see clearly in the dark. If they could bring back part of their past it would be loved ones who have died or time that could have been better spent.

Some of us will choose to age as these wonderful women have. Others will postpone the inevitable, and if we do will need regular touch-ups. I'm not sure which route I'll take or for how long. But something tells me that after thirty years and countless life changes, a smooth face won't match the inner me. I'll look at my image in the mirror and recognize that I have lived every line.

Thank you so much, Rona. I never read these lines without being moved and affected in some significant way.

Some of my most darling friends are in their seventies, eighties, and even nineties. My sweet mother-in-law was ninety-four this year. She experienced the medical miracle of laser surgery on her eyes a few weeks ago.

"Oh, Patricia, when I looked in the mirror I saw there were rivers in my face. I really thought I was looking quite good before the surgery."

Let me tell you something. I personally could look into her eyes and at her face for hours. There is so much beauty there, so much life, so much wisdom, and so much love. She truly epitomizes the merriment of aging. She brings to mind this wonderful, liberating scripture for those of us for whom the years seem to be racing past:

> Like a cedar in Lebanon [majestic, stable, durable, and incorruptible], planted in the house of the LORD, they shall flourish in the courts of our God. [Growing in grace] they shall still bring forth fruit in old age; they shall be full of sap [of spiritual vitality] and [rich in the] verdure [of trust, love and contentment.] [They are living memorials.]
> —Psalm 92:12–14

It's always pleasant to be around someone who is cheerful, even more so if he or she expresses gratitude. Being cheerful and grateful is a workable life-long key. "A happy heart is good medicine and a cheerful mind works healing" (Proverbs 17:22).

As the years unfold, there will be restrictions, limitations, and even losses. Steve and I have happily observed loved ones age with dignity and grace. They hold out to us a baton worth carrying into our own declining years. Never forget, Christ has promised us that new and indestructible bodies await our own resurrections. Maybe we will dance and skip together with bare feet along the banks of His great river. Who would want to be in shoes on streets of transparent gold!

CHAPTER 26

MORE GOOD NEWS: THE BATTLEGROUND OF THE MIND

HAVE YOU EVER thought of your mind as a battleground with cosmic forces clashing for control? Why is the mind so crucial to spiritual progress? Does scripture have anything to say about the mind? Let's lay a few foundation stones!

"And be constantly renewed in the spirit of your mind [having a fresh mental and spiritual attitude]" (Ephesians 4:23).

Greek: *Spirit*—breath, breeze, the rational soul, mental disposition.

In the Greek origins of this word, *mind*, as used biblically, we discover the following:

The mind can be exercised.
The mind can involve our thoughts, feelings, and wills.
The mind knows, resolves and allows.
The mind can be renovated.
The mind involves intelligence.
The mind can be changed and transfigured.
The mind can have deep thoughts and desperate dispositions.

Oxford Dictionary: *Transfigured*—to change, inform, elevate.

Dispositions—bent, natural tendencies, inclination.

Vine's Dictionary of Old and New Testament Words wonderfully defines *the spirit of your mind* as "our new nature which belongs to the believer by reason of the new birth."

- Are you troubled with recurring, unruly thoughts that you want to be rid of?
- Do you battle with disturbing, unsolicited mental activity?
- Do some of your thoughts shock and shame you?
- Do you feel overpowered with negative trends in your thinking?
- Do you find that some well-worn patterns in your mind have a downward, depressing effect on you?

If the mind is a battleground, how can we safely engage in this conflict?

The first issue is to know the enemy. If it is a battle, then there is most certainly an enemy! Scripture gives us a sweeping insight and expose. The combat in the mind is not merely cerebral but spiritual.

> For we are not wrestling with flesh and blood [contending only with physical opponents] but against the despotisms, against the powers, against [the master spirits who are] the world rulers of this present darkness, against the spirit forces of wickedness in the heavenly [supernatural] sphere.
>
> —Ephesians 6:12–17

The raging question is whether we can, by our own abilities and confidence, win this battle or whether it must be fought in the spiritual realm in which we all exist? Do we need someone greater than ourselves? The resounding answer is that Jesus our Creator has Himself the power to renew our minds.

Some destructive patterns of thought are entrenched and found behind tremendous fortifications. Here they are kept "safe and protected" as "strongholds."

Greek: *Strongholds*—to fortify, through the idea of holding safely a castle, a fortress.

Vine's Dictionary defines *strongholds* as "used metaphorically here in Ephesians of those things in which mere human confidence is imposed." Humanism, by definition, is a mindset and lifestyle that begins and ends with man. It is a stronghold of the mind by which people fortify themselves against absolute truth.

The scripture undercuts all such temporary and weak philosophizing with a massive sledgehammer of truth. These fortifications of the mind can only be destroyed by spiritual weaponry.

> For the weapons of our warfare are not physical [weapons of flesh and blood] but they are mighty before God for the overthrow and destruction of strongholds. Inasmuch as we refute arguments, and theories, and reasonings and every proud and lofty thing that sets itself up against the [true] knowledge of God: and we lead every thought and purpose away captive into the obedience of Christ.
> —2 Corinthians 10:4–5

A key battle tactic then is to bring our thoughts—in fact, every thought that sets itself up against God's revealed mind and will—into captivity to obey Christ.

Greek: *Captivity*—to lead away captive a prisoner of war. (So where do we take these captive thoughts? We take them away "to obey Christ.")

Obedience—attention, harkening, submission, to conform to a command or authority, to be obedient to.

Here is the good news. In St. Paul's letter to the Ephesian Christians, we find a blockbuster revelation of what is going on in the invisible world around us. It is so worthwhile to study and understand this passage because it unmasks evil. (See Ephesians 6:10–18.) It reveals God's strategy for us in the conflict against spiritual forces and the devil. God Himself provides a full set of protective armor. In addition, we are given a powerful spiritual weapon that will prove to be 100 percent successful in winning the battle you face in your mind.

This weapon is the Sword of God's Spirit. This is the weapon He personally thrusts and wields in close combat. Why do I say *close combat*? Because the Greek word used here, *machaira*, is a dagger or dirk. Was ever conflict so immediate, so intrusive, so close as when it is in our own minds? This sword is clearly defined as the Word of God, the *rhema* word.

Did you know that God's Spirit speaks individually a *rhema* word to your situation through the inspired written *logos* Word? He gives a specific truth for a specific circumstance. When He does, this very scripture becomes part of your personal relationship and spiritual experience. This may happen as you read or as the Holy Spirit brings to mind, the parts of the Word of God (Logos) which you have stored away.

Accordingly, when in difficulty and under the attack of the devil, you can speak out that specific scripture and divine war begins on your behalf. The Spirit of God takes those very words and thrusts them at your enemies in the spiritual realm as outlined in Ephesians 6.

So why is there such power when Christ speaks through the Holy Spirit? There is of course much that is unsearchable, but we have only to view the night sky from a dark area and remember that "He spoke and the worlds were made." There are more stars than we can mathematically calculate in teeming galaxies, and He calls each one by name. Heavenly bodies like Betelgeuse are so enormous (216 million times the size of the sun by volume) that they defy our capacity to grasp their size.

This creating God is the One Who goes to war in the spiritual realm for His children. The original scriptures were God-breathed through prophets and apostles. When you encounter the Word of God and it is life-giving to your mind and circumstance, something power-packed is happening.

Those will be the very words, when you speak them or write them, that the Spirit of God takes as His own dagger and thrusts at your enemy. Does this sound farfetched? Ask God to speak into your life by His Word about whatever is troubling or threatening you. Then take that Word, believe it and speak it out, and watch God's Holy Spirit go to battle in your behalf.

I have been stunned to discover that many Christians have neither knowledge nor understanding of this powerful weapon. If we personally engage in the Word of God ourselves, all the while giving God's Spirit the opportunity to speak specifically into our circumstances, we don't enter the struggle unarmed.

Let me illustrate very simply. Presently Steve and I are living in a small travel trailer in scenic Banff National Park, Alberta, Canada. We have sold our lovely home in Vancouver and stored our furniture outside of Calgary, where we hope to soon purchase a house. As the weeks pass, there is a certain deep ache, surprisingly strong, a longing to establish a home and again find a more permanent place. One of the primary purposes of simplifying our lives just now is to complete the writing of this book.

By God's prevailing grace, with only enough space for two people to pass in the passage between the bathroom, the eating area, and the bed, we have lived happily for almost three months. There are times, of course, when I can't find what I'm looking for, or when I bang my head on a cupboard door. I confess that my impatience flares almost instantaneously, which, by the way, is a little frightening.

At such times, when I seem beset with yearnings for human stability, for walls on which to hang pictures, for some place to be our own home, I remember a *rhema* word, which I believe the Lord gave us before we arrived here. "And my people shall dwell in a peaceable habitation, and in safe dwellings, and in quiet resting places" (Isaiah 32:18).

Believe me, I know it by heart. When I feel overwhelmed, I speak out this Word, and before I know it my anxiety lifts and my perspective clears. Why is this? The Holy Spirit has taken that scripture and thrust it at the enemy of my soul, who waits tenaciously to steal my joy and peace. "You will keep in perfect peace all who trust in you, whose thoughts are fixed on you!" (Isaiah 26:3).

I wrote a few lines after searching through our garage storage at our son and lovely daughter-in-law's home.

Life's Precious Props

All those acquisitions,
Dreamed up, planned and plotted for.
So many gifts, so much to store.
One by one they stack, each above the other.
It all forms now a high, straight wall,
In someone else's palace hall.

Is this the accumulation of our life?
Significance to identify a husband and his wife?
No, these are the props that will remain,
When the play is over, and the journey done.
They will not measure life's true gain
But, Lord, You know, we've had such fun.

I saw them there, each precious piece, but out of place.
Had these things hindered us in life's long race?
In time, in time, each one again will find
A base for now, to rest, and peace of mind
Someplace we love and call Shalom
A spot upon our planet earth the family will call home.

One of the words almost everyone knows how to spell is *anxiety*. Steve lives on a verse from the epistles. Seriously, it is his meat and drink for all life's vicissitudes.

> Be anxious for nothing but in everything by prayer and supplication with thanksgiving let your requests be made known to God. And the peace of God which surpasses all comprehension shall guard your hearts and your minds in Christ Jesus.
>
> —Philippians 4:6–7 NASB

At the approach of every stress and anxiety, Steve turns to walk in obedience to God by bringing everything in prayer to his heavenly Father. He refers to petition as *begging*, remembers to be thankful, and talks easily about "spelling it all out to God." He really does experience the very peace of God.

A key to military victory is always adequate intelligence. Romans chapter seven helps us understand the state of the battle. There are two laws resident within us. The *law of sin and death* wars against the *law of my mind* and takes me prisoner. The law of my mind serves God.

Understanding these two laws that battle within us at the junction of our choices brings us the freedom we long for. The victory comes from involving Christ. Through Jesus Christ we have been given a principle that drives the supernatural ability to mount a war against the law of sin and death in us and return from the battle with banners flying.

This is because the law of sin resident in my flesh has been overpowered and conquered by the new law of my mind. This new law and power is resident in us by the person of Jesus Christ. He is instantly and continually present in the very life of one who believes in Him and surrenders to Him.

"Do not be conformed to this world, but be transformed by the renewing of your mind, so that you may prove what the will of God is, that which is good and acceptable and perfect" (Romans 12:2 NASB).

Consistent application of these two instructions will progressively strengthen our advance. Let's be strict with ourselves in not conforming! But more positively, we renew our minds by applying time and effort to the scriptures and spending time in the Lord's presence.

A most helpful principle to remember here is that God loves to be first. Scripture teaches that He wants to be first in our finances, our time, and our hearts. There are traces of this in both the Old and New Testaments. So in the morning, if we take a little time quietly in Jesus' presence, it will prove to be the oil that lubricates the whole day. On the other hand, the important thing is not *when* we take the time, but that we do. Working this into an already busy schedule is a challenge, but the strength we receive is worth every effort.

The Ledge

To trust
To put the weight of my whole heart
Down
On what God declares as truth
To flee, with light-speed, from a mind
That twists and turns away, and never again to start
Down those sulphurous canyons of fear and doubt
Where eager perils crouch and roost, awaiting my descent
To depths that strip and steal the deep mysterious peace
That holds me snug and warm against the cold.
Up
On this slender ledge of certain hope.

CHAPTER 27

YOU EXPECT ME TO FORGIVE THIS?

HAVE YOU EVER been betrayed? Gossiped about? Slandered? Why do those dearest have the greatest power to hurt us? Who is among us whose dreams have not been crushed by another? Which of us has a weight of pain beyond our capacity to carry? These questions rise to a crescendo within.

What shall we do? Shall we carry the weight of all these offenses to our graves?

To Forgive or Not to Forgive

Feed not the viper, take no rest,
It longs to feast now in your chest,
On well-accustomed, unforgiven meat,
He beckons you to share and eat.

His acid burns, his venom stings,
Torments more than you can bear
He'd steal your store of precious things
That God supplied for you to share.

There is a cross where you may go
To pour it out, your tale of woe.
A place so safe, you need not hold
It back, a single word, be bold.
Let Him now flush your heart of fear,
For that large space you own so near
Is not as safe as would appear.

Your heart still stores that pain so deep
Such agony, it steals your sleep,
Now Christ's majestic speed and might
Can damn each viper of the night

Admit then life's victorious King
He'll tear away this cursed thing
Fear not, it's He, the crucified
It was for this He bled and died.
In His cold tomb He buried
This ugly weight you've carried.

For if you forgive people their trespasses [their reckless and willful sins, leaving them, letting them go, and giving up resentment], your heavenly Father will also forgive you. But if you do not forgive others their trespasses [their reckless and willful sins, leaving them, and letting them go, and giving up resentment], neither will your Father forgive you your trespasses.

—Matthews 6:14–15

Matthew 6 is teaching us that if we forgive, we will be forgiven. If we do not forgive, we will not be forgiven. This is rather stark when we consider life's wounds. Yet when the disciples asked Jesus to teach them how to pray, the subject of forgiving and being forgiven was woven into the very center of the Lord's Prayer. "As we forgive those who have trespassed against us" (Matthew 6:12).

Would you like to copy out the three verses above in your own notebook and allow the Holy Spirit to burn them deep into your mind and heart? We do our personal dance around our demands for a certain standard of sorrow over sins committed against us. All the while we leave the sinner clearly outside the circle of our hearts' boundaries. We so easily can turn from our own transgressions, freely forgiven, to feed the inferno of anger toward anyone who has lacerated us.

There is a glimpse of lavish love found in The Gospel of Luke, chapter seven. Simon, one of the Pharisees, invited Jesus to his home for a meal. His motive was unclear, only we find him extremely condemning of a certain woman of ill repute who slips, uninvited, into his feast. Perhaps they were dining in the great outdoors beside his house. Here we are somehow unable to tie forgiveness down to a legal formula. As expected, Jesus swept away Simon's self-righteous hypocrisy.

This lady was notorious and had undoubtedly sinned against men and women alike in the community. With a treasured alabaster flask of expensive perfume, she positioned herself at Christ's feet. He was her only destination. It is not at all surprising to me that in the presence of Jesus she was overcome with weeping. Getting close to Him will do that to you. All the shame, all the sorrow, all the rejection spilled out liquid in His presence.

Was she suddenly embarrassed that her tears were falling onto His feet? Then she knelt on the hard stone, wiping them from His feet with her hair. The room was electrified. Some wondered whether there would be an outpouring of sordid confessions. Others were disgusted at her presence, her forwardness toward the celebrated guest of the evening.

Every eye was on her, even the servants had scurried in to watch the episode. Shock ripped through the room as she pulled the stopper on the extravagant perfume and began to pour it over Christ's feet, all the while affectionately kissing them. Still she did not speak.

Simon the host exploded inwardly with highly charged and judgmental thoughts that discredited Christ and despised this woman "devoted to sin." Jesus, knowing fully Simon's thoughts, addressed him.

"A certain lender of money [at interest] had two debtors; one owed him five hundred denarii, and the other fifty. When they had no means of paying, he freely forgave them both. Now which of them will love him more?"

Simon answered, "The one, I take it, for whom he forgave and canceled more."

And Jesus said to him, "You have decided correctly."

Then turning toward the woman, he said to Simon, "Do you see this woman? When I came into your house you gave me no water for my feet, but she has wet my feet with her tears and wiped them with her hair. You gave me no kiss, but she, from the moment I came in, has not ceased [intermittently] to kiss my feet tenderly and caressingly. You did not anoint my head with [cheap, ordinary] oil, but she has anointed my feet with [costly, rare] perfume. Therefore I tell you, her sins, many as they are, are forgiven her because she has loved much. But he, who is forgiven little, loves little."

And He said to her, "Your sins are forgiven!"

Tonight I imagined that cleansed and transformed woman rising from the flagstone floor and walking away from the feast. Despite the presence of so many, this had been life's most private moment for her. Oh, that she could be invisible in this hour with all their eyes piercing her as she made her exit. But all her shame had drained away; she had been cleansed by the Master and Maker of all creation. She tasted the sweet and satisfying drink of forgiveness. She carried her alabaster flask, empty, into the night; yet her heart was full to bursting with love for the Christ of God. She could never be the same. As she made her way out into the village street, all the rest of her life rose to greet her.

The truth about all of our debts—our sins against heaven and man—is that we have no means with which to pay, no means whatsoever. What shall we give in exchange for our souls? If there was, in fact, some stash of gold bars or some means of personal sacrifice, then Christ would not have needed to be crucified. There is but one payment in the entire universe that will suffice for the tiniest toxic spot on our souls. Truthfully, the pervasiveness of our personal sins has so engulfed us that there are no unblemished areas.

"The heart is deceitful above all things and desperately wicked; who can know it?" (Jeremiah 17:9 NKJV).

"For all have sinned and fall short of the glory of God" (Romans 3:23 NKJV).

Not one soul in the human race is excluded from the divine sentence against sin. No man or woman has the currency to pay the debt of sin against a holy God. In the eternity of eternities a Lamb is seen as freshly slain. His blood will speak forgiveness and acceptance to us through the endless ages. Tell me now, what are these arguments and excuses we contrive against extending forgiveness to others?

Having recently returned home from Europe, I stood in my mother's kitchen, stoutly declaring that there was someone I never wanted to see again. In her wise and quiet way she asked if I would go for a walk and tell the Lord that I was willing for Him to make me willing to forgive.

Turning over her entreaty in my mind, I decided that I could at least do that. So I walked out, and in a field of spreading grasses, I prayed, *Lord, I am willing to be made willing to forgive.*

It was less than a month later when the very person I never wanted to see again came striding straight across a room to me at an anniversary celebration in another city. He extended his hand to me and said these words, "Is all forgiven?" Without hesitation, the words tumbled from my mouth, "Of course, Dad."

For many subsequent years and even to the last year of his life, I enjoyed the sweet fruit of that reconciliation. Thank you, Mom, for the simple phrase, "willing to be made willing." I have passed it on to many who were struggling to forgive.

So what does forgiveness look like? Here are some defining elements.

Greek: *Forgiveness*—to send forth, to forsake, to lay aside, to leave, to let [alone], to remit [to pardon], to omit, to yield up.

Oxford Dictionary: *Send forth*—bid go.

(This is your first line of defense. You refuse to give the offense space in your mind.)

Forsake—abandon, give up, break off from, withdraw one's help. (Remember, the devil needs your compliance in nursing offenses.)

Thesaurus: *Lay aside*—finish with, give up (visualize actually bundling up the offense and sin against you and deliberately laying it down at Christ's cross and walking away from it.)

Oxford Dictionary: *Leave*—abstain from consuming or dealing with.

Let alone—allow or cause (the offense) to be solitary.

Remit—refrain from exacting or executing a debt or punishment. (No subtle backhanding or retaliation. No more grinding the guilty into the dirt.)

Omit—leave out, neglect. (This speaks to me of a deliberate choice to leave out of mind, memory, or speech another's trespass and no longer to give any attention to it.)

Yield up—give up, deliver over, surrender. (Again, this puts forgiveness in the neon lights.)

I have discovered that these definitions are wonderfully strength-giving when battling with the need to forgive.

The questions rocket to the surface of the mind. Do you mean this is how I should handle:

- insults?
- betrayal?
- slander?
- a breaking heart?
- my out-of-control attitudes?
- the onslaught of memories?
- the periodic irrepressible pain?

As I write these questions, I'm beginning a list you will want to add to. I am reminded of a powerful and wealthy leper in the Old Testament.

Naaman was commander of the army of Syria. During one of his raids he had brought back captive a young girl from the land of Israel. She became a servant to Naaman's wife. The maid told her of a prophet in Samaria who would heal Naaman's leprosy.

Remember, God always has His man, His woman, strategically positioned for the purpose of His glory. Even the king of Syria, who held his commander in high esteem, got involved, bypassing the prophet and going directly to the king of Israel. Israel's king received the letter from the king of Syria telling him to heal Naaman of leprosy. He tore his clothes and asked, "Am I a god to kill and make alive?"

Elijah heard of the king's distress and sent word, "Let him come to me and he shall know that there is a prophet in Israel."

In due time, Naaman arrived with chariot and horses at Elijah's door. He was expecting the prophet to appear, call on the name of the Lord, and wave his hand over the leprous places. No, Elijah sent a simple, straightforward command via his servant, "Go and wash in the Jordan River seven times and your flesh shall be restored to you, and you shall be clean."

Perhaps Naaman was insulted or indignant at the simplicity of the instruction. He growled excuses about better rivers in his own land and stormed away in a rage. As he traveled, his own servants entreated him, "If the prophet had told you to do something great, would you not have done it? How much more then, when he says to you, 'Wash and be clean'?

Finally he went down to the Jordan River and dipped himself seven times. As promised, his whole body became as fresh as a little child's (2 Kings 5:1–14).

So what is my point about forgiving? Simply this, to be free ourselves we need to follow the directions. If we will take these defining elements of forgiveness, speak them out, and by God's grace enact them, we will discover the miraculous power of heaven on our side. That powerful urge to build *legitimate* resistance to forgiveness will curl up and die.

"No way," you say. "Too simple. This cursed leprous thing that clings to my very flesh needs more than that." Dare to humble yourself before God—if need be, fifty times a day—in this mortal struggle. I promise you the devil will slink away every time in the face of your costly obedience and the authority of the Word of God against him.

Just this week I was discussing forgiveness with my lovely cousin, Rosella. She opined that our Lord's discourse about forgiving seventy times seven times helps us when the offenses rear up again and again in our minds.

Here are three scriptures that trample on the serpent's head.

"Behold I have given you authority and power to trample upon serpents and scorpions, and [physical and mental strength and ability] over all the power that the enemy [possesses]; and nothing shall in any way harm you" (Luke 10:19).

[God is speaking here] "For I will forgive their iniquity, and their sin I will remember no more" (Jeremiah 31:34 NKJV).

"Therefore be imitators of God as dear children. And walk in love, as Christ has loved us and given Himself for us" (Ephesians 5:1–2 NKJV).

If we connect the last two verses, we will imitate Him. Does this seem too simplistic against your weight of indignation and pain? I have found the combination of these definitions and these scriptures to be a razor-sharp weapon to sever this sinful unforgiveness from my heart. The instructions are simple, and the results are spectacular!

Freely Forgive

Tell me, "Where is true forgiveness found?"
It's found on blood-drenched holy ground.
For God alone can guilt dispel
He slammed for us the gates of hell,
A cross impaled creation's King
His bruising wounds our healing bring.

Our every sin was swept away
Into His sacrifice that day.
God's righteous wrath will never come,
It fell upon His well-loved Son.
All the memories, all the shame
Christ embraced, He took the blame.
There buried far beyond our reach
His mercy we may now beseech.

Our Father chooses to forget.
Foul accusations here are met.
From broken body, poured out blood
Forgiveness comes, a rushing flood
A welcome call, a banquet spread,
He serves a feast of wine and bread.

So shall I keep my grudge so strong
Against the one who did me wrong?
Remembering not my own huge debt
By Christ's great sacrifice is met
Oh, teach me, Lord, now mercy's way,
Trespasses to forgive each day.
Allow me to release this pain
Refuse to take it up again.

Here standing strong, my soul so free
On eagle wings I fly to Thee
With gratitude for evermore
Oh, Christ my God, I do adore
Your passion spent forgiving me
I do now all my debtors free.

CHAPTER 28

KEEP A LIGHT ON THE STAIRS

"Her lamp does not go out, but it burns on continuing
through the night [of trouble privation or sorrow,
warning away fear, doubt and distrust]"
—Proverbs 31:18

THE WORD *NIGHT* in the Hebrew figuratively means adversity. Her candle is not blown out by adversity. She has resources, confidence in her God, and welcome at her gate, her door, her heart. When someone close and dear to you is in spiritual or other peril, keep your door ajar and always a light on the stair. Why? To welcome the wounded, the hurting, the wayward, and the prodigal. Jesus comes to bless in the most unsuspecting ways when we see every human being in the dignity with which God has crowned them.

Samantha used to drink way too much and was sleeping with her boyfriend. She had a Christian background and had wandered a long way away. Pregnant, she discovered she was not his only conquest! In due time, a baby girl arrived with all the legal and emotional complications with the father. Much care and sensitivity is needed to be any help at all at such a time.

Fast forward six years and you would be amazed. Samantha is a wonderful mother, and the baby, now six, a delightful bundle of life. But you would weep if you could hear this sweet sister praying for me. Now in my low times she rises with great strength and resources.

Have a well-stocked heart ready for such times; for they will surely come to you and to those you love. I cannot bypass my own vulnerability when it comes to being available. I have to confess that often my first response to need is resistance. Truly, I am ashamed to tell you so. Oh, how often the Lord has needed to give me a changed heart, a willing heart. It seems to me that needs and other such opportunities present themselves at most inconvenient times. My reactions are shortsighted and selfish, yet the Lord is so gracious in His mercy to tune my heart to His. The magnitude of the privilege and the rewards, some secret and a few open, are without earthly calculation.

Our journey as a couple, and as a family, has been full of such privilege. Jesus has come to our door in one form or another, and I must tell you that we have gained dearest and deepest life friendships.

Uncle Walter was a war veteran. He began in North Africa, when he was not yet twenty. Over eighteen months he walked almost the whole length of Italy—during a burning summer between two of the nastiest winters on record. In the Po Valley a shell exploded close to his head, blowing out his eardrum on one side and shattering his cranium. Remarkably, he lived and was evacuated, first to England, and later, by ship, to Halifax. The next several years were spent having endless reconstructive surgeries, mostly done in Vancouver, British Columbia, far away from friends and family.

Walter drank. Through the seemingly endless convalescence, he drank to forget, he drank for the pain and the loneliness. In fact, for many years his military disability pension was converted into fine Scottish whiskey and shared with a few cronies. Some months he was rolled and dried out for a time. His precise military appearance gave way to chronic cirrhosis, a scabbing skin disease. In the fierce Alberta winters he often slept at the base of the vast incinerator at the lumber mill, where we found him once in very poor shape. The doctor recommended bathing him in coal tar and sobering him up.

There were two Walters. For six weeks he appeared at breakfast in the morning in a pressed shirt and every hair in place. He read stories to our little ones, who loved him and clambered all over him. They were fascinated with some of the tubular arrangements in his head that connected one of his ears to a nasal cavity. Walter was helpful around the home and cheerful.

Then the cravings would overwhelm him, and he went back to the liquor, back on the street, back to sleeping in the soot. We would let some time pass and then go look for him. In later years he had both legs amputated because of dreadful circulation issues. We all loved him, and in his very last months my brother Ted led him in a sinner's prayer.

There will be an abundance of opportunity for you, under the careful guidance of the Holy Spirit, to bring forth treasures old and new from your reserve. You can make your home a refuge for those who wander alone in the cold nights of their lives.

How do we reach out to such in our broken world? Whenever possible, use the scripture for encouragement. It is, indeed, supernatural. I have a darling sister who gives me a scripture whenever she phones. This is not casual; she has prayed and talked to the Lord about it first. It is always a strength.

It was challenging at first to pray with people I didn't know well—believers and unbelievers. Something amazing happens when we pray with another. I am convinced it is because we enter together into an open heaven, and both of us are there in the throne room of the universe, in the presence of the King. Always ask permission, and then rely on the Holy Spirit to lead you as you pray. People invariably thank me, and sometimes they cry. They may surprise you and pray themselves! I remember while receiving a facial at a spa school, a lovely young lady began to open her life to me. I asked if I could pray for her. She said that I could.

My eyes were covered with patches, and the room was full of murmuring instructors, students, and clients. I prayed a simple prayer and after the amen she was very quiet.

"Are you OK?" I asked.

"Yes," she said, "but you made me cry."

"No," I said, "it's nothing to do with me. It's God's Holy Spirit moving in your heart."

Never underestimate the power of reaching out to God with the simplest prayer for another human being.

"A good man [woman] out of the good treasure of her heart brings forth what is good, and an evil man [woman] out of the evil treasure, brings forth what is evil, for her mouth speaks from that which fills her heart." (Luke 6:45).

Hold your treasures lightly, in case the Lord has need of them. "For where your treasure is, there will your heart be also" (Luke 12:34).

At the same time, there must be a balance between our service and availability to the needy and our personal and family needs. Refreshment and recreation are important in life's journey. Take a rest. Periodically pull up the drawbridge of your castle. Prepare a favorite meal. Close the drapes, light the candles, shut off the phone, and enjoy the leisurely beauty of only the family.

God bless you as you struggle to find the balance point between laying down your life in sacrifice for the needs of others and retreating to your own family circle.

Periodically, amid much joy and privilege, the counterpoints have left us winded, myself personally, our marriage, and even our church community. There is a holy and divine tension in life that brings both joy and sorrow. Under God this provides a delicate and safe balance between pride and despair. The harmony produced in the melody of the one affecting the other becomes the music of living.

At one such time, when adversity lashed like a vicious storm against our family, I wrote the following lines. Perhaps they will reach you now or on some future day.

How Many Storms

How many storms can one family survive?
At the end of the blast will we still be alive?
Tyrannical tempests on our castle's gate
Fears are now rising, the hour is late.

We pray to our Father, to bring us release
"From fracture and turmoil, please bring your peace.
To hearts that are knit, so close and so true,
Bonds thought unbreakable, come, Jesus, do.
Be the refuge we need in this time of distress,
All our lives are before you, our sins we confess.

Our roots are far-reaching, so strong and so deep
Promises we made then, we work now to keep.
Ruthless the demons in shadows so near.
Our cries ever rising, we beg You to hear."

He comes, oh, so sudden, with speed lightning fast,
He'll speak to the tempest, He'll silence the blast.
Our hearts are now quiet; the fear leaves no trace,
We rest in the grip of His holy embrace.

"For you have been a stronghold for the poor, a stronghold for the needy in his distress, a shelter from the storm, a shade from the heat; for the blast of the ruthless ones is like a rainstorm against a wall" (Isaiah 25:4).

There are times when a spouse, a child, or a friend seems totally unreachable. There is remoteness, even a hardening in heart matters. Something huge and impassable has risen between you. The walls are too high to scale. Your own heart breaks with strong surges of helplessness. One once so close now seems so distant.

Consider, for a few moments, how the one behind the un-scalable fortress feels. Does he or she feel uncertain, insecure, and desolate in the aloneness of soul struggles? They have heard you call out their name, recognizing the reality in your voice, and yet they feel powerless to respond in kind.

"What is going on?" you ask. Could it be that the King of the entire universe, Who died to be King of our hearts, patiently waits for us to turn to Him for help, for them and for ourselves?

The psalmist, King David, wrote, "Bow your heavens, O LORD, and come down … stretch forth your hand from above; rescue me and deliver me" (Psalm 144:5, 7).

Could we transliterate this verse as "Please roll up your sleeves and help us"?

David needed God to act, and at such times, so do we. We can pray the psalmist's prayer, and see the fortification crumble in His presence and at His voice.

The subsequent rubble that surrounds your loved one will be no hindrance to their freely walking out with Him. Everyone's passage to God's heart is his or her own personal journey. Filling out our role in obedience is so often key to a fortress being torn down.

Ours is to pray, to love, to believe, to wait.

For John

A distant echo beats upon my fortress walls,
A voice so foreign, yet familiar and persistent, calls.
So far away yet now so near, inside I feel a rising fear.
To run, to hide, in some small space
Where sounds like this could find no place
To reach me in my well planned world.
Yet growing doubts around me swirled.
This call now reaches deeps in me,
A crack is forming, I can see
A cross-shaped blast of light on me.

So all I feared from God above
Is melted down by heat of love,
Poured out in blood of Christ for me,
He'll take my hand, I'll walk out free.

CHAPTER 29

MY TIME FOR SURGERY

BEING RUSHED TO surgery was both scary and relieving. I had noticed something abnormal about my breathing. Two thousand miles from home, and working at a conference center in the Muskoka Lakes, Ontario to help put myself through the next year of college, it had become completely impossible to breathe through my nose. A strong round-the-clock dose of antibiotic was prescribed over several weeks, but it had no effect. The bewildered doctor decided to send me to a specialist, who was also a surgeon.

This brilliant Jewish doctor, in turn, fired me off to emergency and scheduled immediate surgery. Somewhere I had contracted a condition that he had seen only once before in his profession, and it was on a boxer's face!

Post-operatively the medical staff were tremendous but would not allow me to look in a mirror. The bridge of my nose had been eaten away to a fragile shell, and the timing of the surgery was just hours before my nose would have collapsed on my face. Not a pretty prospect for a young lady!

Many years later it felt as if it was time for surgery again. This time it had nothing to do with my health or my body, but God was about to perform a wonderful surgery on my heart. Of course, surgery is never convenient, nor is it usually welcomed. For me it was mandatory—at least it seemed that way as far as God was concerned.

Insecurity had taken such a hold that it made me beyond frustration to live with. Basically, it was the result of my inability to trust and my feelings of inadequacy. Trust, of course, is integral to a good marriage, and many women struggle with various insecurities regarding themselves and their husbands. Some feel insecure about their appearance, their weight, their social skills, or their material and financial state. Some struggle over their husbands, his good looks, his popularity, his past, his habits, his capacity to spend money, and any number of other such issues.

One sleepless night I slipped out of bed and went down to the family room. I literally rolled in an agony in front of the fireplace. The Lord was, in mercy, taking the lid off my heart, and I was discovering that I had the power to destroy everything valuable in my life. Steve, out of desperation, had told me that if I didn't start pulling it together he would send me back to my mother. He wasn't serious, but they were troubled months.

I needed to take hold of my self-destructive path and choose to make an effort, but I felt powerless to change. I became insecure at the slightest provocation.

Then, when beginning to heal from the self-inflicted emotional wounding I inevitably pulled at the healing scab. That late night by the fireplace, in anguish before God, deep surgery was taking place. He was gently drawing me into Himself, and into the knowledge that my deepest security was in Him.

Afterwards came the long convalescence that lasted for about eighteen months, and so began the journey of discovery as to what Jesus Christ had achieved for me personally in His death and resurrection. During this time, the Lord gave me a picture that startlingly portrayed this chapter of my life. There was a high cliff. The edges fell precipitously, plunging to dangerous pits below. Sloping toward that cliff edge were well-worn rutted paths. They were acutely familiar; I had been there often, and I could describe them in detail. As soon as I stepped on one of them, I was all but gone down the well-greased slope to the waiting pits. These were places of isolation and insecurity; they reeked of helplessness.

Jesus showed me that He would be there at the precipice edge for me. He would block my way to failure and destruction by His presence. At every point of personal damage and weakness He would hold me. At every place of vulnerability, which Satan so readily took advantage of, He was there for me. For every sin committed, for every rebellious act, He was there, taking the full punishment in Himself. My incalculable sin debt was paid for by His suffering and death. The payment to deliver me from death was to be in blood—His blood. He showed me that the self-destructive bent in me, beyond my ability to control, was taken into His own body in crucifixion. There it was delivered a death blow, and now I must live in the light of that actual fact. He showed me that whenever I was overwhelmed by fears He would be there twenty-four/seven; those dreadful pits could be history.

I also learned during the many months of recovery that I would continually need Him because the cliff edge would be there for the rest of my life. Beyond the precipice edge He had planted endless grasslands for me, and mountains rose in beckoning splendor. There, too, flowed the River of Life. His invitation was to explore His goodness, His power, and His love.

"But you have lovingly delivered my soul from the pit of corruption, for you have cast all my sins behind your back" (Isaiah 38:17 NKJV).

It soon became apparent that the Lord planned to win on the battleground of my mind. He became very strict with me relating to my thought life. If one suspicious, untrusting thought was given momentary occupancy, I was hurtling down those well-oiled ruts again. I had to learn the meaning and the relevance of St. Paul's instruction, "Bringing every thought into captivity to the obedience of Christ" (2 Corinthians 10:5).

I discovered I was not going to make it on my own. I had previously been the primary one giving counsel and offering prayer in any given situation. Now I knew it was I who needed the prayers and support of others.

I will never forget returning from a trip to another city with my mother. As we neared our home I invited her in to join us for the evening meal. When we drove into the garage, I felt myself being drawn by a great enticing magnet to one of those familiar ruts. I immediately asked my mother to pray for me. In her own sweet simplicity she offered an uncomplicated prayer. The darkness lifted tangibly from my heart and mind.

Since that period of time I have readily asked for the prayers of others. Jesus Christ was circling me and reining me in to a closeness and dependence on Him and His people that I had never known before. I was learning that, although we live in such an intensely self-sufficient generation, we have a fundamental and irreversible need of each other.

CHAPTER 30

OH, GOD, WHAT DOES THIS MEAN?

YOU HAVE BEEN patient and persistent to travel with me in this book. Does putting these things into practice feel remote? Perhaps to use the keys now on your key ring seems impossible in your life experience. If you were momentarily to peer through one of the keyholes in your castle, what do you think you would see? There is a cross, rugged and stained with blood. Here, and here only, are the complete answers to our questions and objections. This is where we will find the power to take ownership and begin to live life from our new residence.

Your key ring is heavy with keys. You have visited many rooms in your castle, but the reality of living there would mean so many changes. In fact, spending time with Prudence, Discretion, and Virtue right now would certainly be a challenge.

Quite suddenly you realize Someone is standing beside you. He speaks with soothing tenderness, reaching out His hand for yours. You cannot help but notice the long, deep scar penetrating through His hand. You hear His voice, so gentle yet so compelling, "Come and follow Me, I've taken care of everything."

The way to the castle of our inheritance is, first and last, by way of the cross. As we draw to a close in this book, I confess that I am not a theologian, nor do I bring you the advantages of scholarship. I must, however, tell you in the simplest of terms what Jesus achieved, personally, for you and me in His crucifixion over two thousand years ago. You may be asking, "What does this really mean?"

It means that there is no sin so deep or dark that Christ did not take the punishment for it in His own human body. Christ's death is supremely effective in the transfer of all my guilt to Himself. This powerful, mysterious transaction leaves me clean, completely cleansed by His blood. (See 1 John 1:9.) Now nothing hinders our friendship with God.

You may ask, "What can I do for Him? He has suffered so much for me." Believe in Him; trust in what He has finished for you; turn from all the things that are sinful and defiling; commit your entire future on earth and all of eternity to the care of this magnificent Savior.

What is the crucial result of this? When our memories bring up our sins, now fully confessed and forgiven, there is no obligation to them, nor is there space in our lives for them. They were carried away by Christ forever when He died. He and God the Father have chosen to forget them. So can you. Those haunting specters of your past and mine are completely forgotten. Why not skip and dance at the wonder of this?

Jesus now leads us to a window seat in your castle. He points to the distance. We follow the direction of His hand. Clearly outlined on the skyline are three crosses. Daylight is diminishing, and although it is high noon, it seems that night has come unexpectedly.

"Come with me for a few moments," He invites, "before we share a meal together."

Suddenly we feel irregular rock under our feet. Our eyes are looking at something we could never have imagined. In full view, we see Him, Jesus, nailed through hands and feet, and hanging between earth and sky. The agony and anguish are indescribable. We are rooted to the ground in frightful horror at such suffering. Then, strangely, we see ourselves. We are dressed in filthy garments, and we are right up there on that cross with Him. Oh, my God, what does this mean? Me? Why am I up there?

"I am crucified with Christ" (Galatians 2:20).

Is it from the cross, or is His voice beside us? We hear someone speaking. "I took you into my own death with me, for only death could deal with everything in you that is poised to destroy you." This was far more than we can take in, yet even in this fearfully awesome place we feel peace, and we know it is coming straight from His presence deeply into our hearts.

Soon a giant scroll begins to unroll before our eyes. We are spectators, fully aware of being shielded by a divine presence. Strength drains out of our bodies; there is a powerful twisting and gliding serpent that assaults the cross before us. With inconceivable speed, the head of that horrible monster is crushed by the deadly thrust of a majestic heel. Christ's own heel, now bruised, is fully intact, yet the snake lies in a conquered heap. There is lightning in the sky above us. The earth heaves and trembles beneath our feet. Momentarily, we see all the hosts of hell, every dark creature, being led across the universe in an open panorama of total defeat. Every one of them is now Christ's vanquished prisoner.

We watch as two well-dressed figures take Jesus' dead and battered body down from the cross. They are both wealthy men and secret followers. Nicodemas brings the burial spices in abundance; Joseph donates his tomb. It is a new tomb cut into the rocky hillside for his own later use.

They wrap the still-pale form in fine linen for burial. Pilate, the Roman governor, assured by the centurion that Jesus had been dead for some time, has given this courageous Joseph permission to take the body down and bury it. We, shaken by the earthquake, chilled by the night air and stunned by the unfolding drama, follow. If we didn't both see it with our own eyes, we would have doubted what happens next.

We see ourselves lying beside Jesus on the cold slab. Then, slowly, a great stone is rolled across the entrance. The words keep running through our heads with great intensity. "With me in my death, buried with me in my tomb." *Oh, my God, what can this mean?*

With loud rumbling and violent breaking of rocks, the scene changes. In a flash of morning glory there is an angel seated on the stone and the tomb is open. (See Matthew 28:3.) We intuitively know that this is now the third day.

There He is, radiant and alive, outside the tomb. Stunned and joyful, we watch. Overwhelmed by His resurrection, we almost miss ourselves in the picture, now robed totally in white. In later weeks we would figure that this was the exchange, His righteousness for our sins. There we are beside Him. *Oh, my God, what does this mean?* Across the thousands of years, various words from the New Testament come on the morning air, mingling with the dawn chorus, "I am crucified with Christ. Buried with Him in His death. risen to newness of life."

Without actually realizing how we got back to the window seat of your castle, we are both delighted to hear Jesus invite us again to join Him for a meal in an intimate dining room. Virtue seems to appear out of nowhere and lead the way. A heavy mahogany door opens into a gently lit room, and in it is a bountiful table. We are famished and filled with wonder at this unexpected treat, to actually sit and have a sumptuous meal with Jesus.

Questions flood our minds; they could keep, or could they? A gentle silence envelops us. Discretion and Prudence drift in and out, caring for our every conceivable need. I can't help but notice the knowing glance that passes between you and Prudence. You are already becoming friends. You break the silence with a quiet question.

Turning to Jesus you ask Him, "Tell me, are you really God?" His answer is both thrilling and pulsating with life. "I am the First and the Last, the Alpha and the Omega. I am the One Who was, Who is, and Who is to come. I am the Lord God Almighty. I am the Lamb of God, sacrificed to pay for your sins; I am your peace and protection, your help in times of need. I am your fortress and your tower of defense, and your eternal life. You can leave all your problems with me to work out. Nothing is impossible with me."

You are drinking in His every word, and so am I. It is all so comfortable and easy in His presence. It feels so safe, so secure. Oh, how we want this time to go on forever.

The girls are discretely clearing the table. Now only the fruit of the vine and the remains of the bread are left from the meal.

His eyes, deep and solemn, turn on us with such unspeakable love in them. He takes the loaf and breaks a piece of it. He passes it to you, and then a piece to me. "This is my body, broken for you. Eat and don't forget Me."

We could never doubt Him again as He reaches for the cup. Once more we see the deep scars through His hands.

"This is my blood shed for you for the sending away of your sins. Drink, and remember Me."

The warmth and nearness of His presence flood our beings. I turn and notice Discretion enter the room. I thought of a burning question I needed to ask Him, but He was gone, and there was a ring of keys on the table.

Astounded at the rapid changes of scene and the moving events at dinner, we walk slowly back to the now familiar window. In the distance you see it first, high and suspended, a colossal and magnificent city. We both know it is our final destination.

APPENDIX

STAGGERING TRANSFORMATION BY JENNIE

I MET DAN in Winnipeg. He was going to Bible school with my sister Laura Lea. I drove out to the school one Friday night to visit her. I ended up meeting him, and we went for a ride in my yellow Jeep. We became fast friends.

A few months later he asked me if I would consider dating him, and we dated long-distance for about ten months. Then I moved in order be near him.

Our relationship had a few ups and downs, but mostly I just knew that Dan was the man I wanted to marry. I couldn't imagine being with anyone else. Four years later, we were married, and I loved my wedding day. It was everything I had dreamed of.

While we were on our honeymoon, a few things occurred that gave me my first taste of how it felt to be treated like less than a queen. I didn't like it, and it confused me, but I didn't know how to verbalize my misgivings.

I got over it and mostly enjoyed our honeymoon. Our first year of marriage wasn't nearly as hard as I had been told it would be. We both brought into it our unique brand of dysfunction, and while it wasn't perfect all the time, I really didn't have too much to complain about.

By the end of year two we had established a pattern of unhealthy ways to deal with conflict. I was the angry, need-to-work-it-out-right-now, I-don't-care-how-loud-it-gets conflict resolution person, and Dan was the hide-in-my-cave, wait-till-the-storm-blows-over-and-never-speak-about-it-again person.

I was often dealt the silent treatment, and I distinctly remember one time that he did not speak one word to me for two weeks. When he finally started speaking to me again and I questioned him, he wasn't able to tell me why. Sometimes he couldn't even remember why he had given me the silent treatment, or possibly he was too afraid to tell me because it would set off a new argument.

By year three we were two extremely selfish people just trying to get our needs met. We were not having any real successes on the marriage front. I can honestly say that it never once occurred to me to check my Bible and obey what it said, and yet we attended church every week as well as a midweek Bible study. We both had said the sinner's prayer at some time in our lives, so as far as we were concerned, we were Christians. If you had asked others who knew us, they probably would have said we were basically good people. We even tried to have devotional lives but mostly failed at that and ended up going months and months on end without ever opening the scriptures for ourselves.

Obviously, we had never learned to communicate our hearts to one another. By year four it had become very bad. Because we had both grown up in the church, we knew enough of the Bible to be able to preach to anyone about the big things a person should not do, but we were not in the Word, learning how to live day by day.

God has a lot to say to married people, and I largely ignored this teaching because it was inconvenient for me to submit to him. I was fiercely independent, and it seemed futile and useless for him to love me as Christ loved the church and sacrificed Himself for her. So he didn't do his part, and I didn't do mine. We lived like two strangers in the same space. Roommates have better relationships than we did as husband and wife.

It would cause him physical pain if I raised my voice, but I refused to find a new way to communicate because I had determined that he was not going to change me. He made repeated requests for me to please not speak to him that way, and I made repeated requests for him to stop nagging me.

Eventually we gave up trying to communicate altogether. We spoke just enough to be able to get the bills paid.

I was a customer service representative at an electronics company. I was all sweetness and light at work. I dealt with a lot of irate people and ironically became known as the person who could talk down any customer and send him or her on their way with a smile.

I couldn't communicate with my own husband but could charm my customers, no matter how angry they were. I was one person at work and a completely different person at home.

There was a married man at work who had been paying attention to me, making sure to show up in the kitchen when I came in for my coffee in the morning. He listened to me and made me laugh. It was right at the time in my marriage that I had given up any hope of ever being understood or having my needs met. Eventually he made a clear move on me; I knew a line had been crossed, that it wasn't just flirting anymore. It was a Friday. I went home and obsessed about him. I allowed my mind to travel anywhere it wanted to, and by Monday morning I was ready to indicate my willingness to meet with him "just to talk." Just talking turned into an affair that lasted for four years. I continued to play nice at work, I continued to show up at home every night and pretend. I lived a total lie, still going to church on Sunday and showing up at Bible study. I became the great pretender.

In order to pull this off, I withdrew from all meaningful relationships. I didn't return phone calls to my family for fear that they would somehow figure it out; I didn't have a single close relationship with another woman. I became a master liar. I lied about everything, even stuff I didn't have to lie about. It became a way of life.

I was asked a few times by this man to leave Dan. He said he would leave his family. He had a wife and daughter when we started our affair and his wife got pregnant and they had a second child while we were still together. I wanted to leave with him but something held me back. I just couldn't figure out how the people-pleaser in me would be able to do this without having people think poorly of me. So I kept putting him off. I went through moments of supreme anguish and hopelessness as I tried to juggle both lives.

Particularly difficult times of each day were the moments of waking and the time I spent trying to fall asleep. These were times when I was overcome with my sin, so I prayed and promised God that tomorrow I would stop. When I woke up in the morning, I was resolved to live that day differently, but by the time I arrived at work, I didn't feel quite so bad about myself and would dive right back in where I left off.

Eventually, while I was still seeing this man, I changed jobs and started going to the gym. It was there that I found and became involved with a second man. He did not know anything about the first. I sort of dumped the first to be with the second. I was sure that I was in love with this man. He was a single father and he needed me, and so did his five-year-old son. At least that's the lie I told myself. So began a new round of secrets and lies.

I also began a more intense round of resolve to stop this behavior and become the best wife and best Christian I could be. I sometimes went as long as six months without any contact with either of my lovers, but then would come a point of need, another huge miscommunication with Dan, or another round of the silent treatment, and I would return, sometimes seeing both men during the same time period. At one point both of them were asking me to leave Dan so that I could be with them.

Eventually I added a third man to the list. He was very sick emotionally and he too "needed" me. For six years I had to keep all of my lies straight, trying to dream up excuses for why I was not home when I should be. There were times when I thought I might actually be going insane.

I finally came to a breaking point and decided enough was enough. I couldn't confess, because where would that leave me? Everyone would think poorly of me, and I just couldn't have that. I couldn't tell my husband. I couldn't go to God because I distinctly recall a conversation I had with one of my lovers that by choosing to live the way I was, I was choosing to go to hell.

I was hopeless. I was sick of living a lie. I was tired of trying to be good when I always ended up in worse sin than before. I made up my mind that the only thing I could really do was disappear. So I applied for a one-year work and travel visa for Brazil.

When it was approved, I reserved a flight and decided not to tell Dan anything, just leave him a note saying that I wouldn't be back, so he should move on and not wait for me.

Shortly before I was set to leave, I was on a weekend trip to one of the Thousand Islands and I got alone and started writing. Somehow, in that moment, it became clear to me that if I ever wanted to be free in Brazil, I would need to tell the truth. So I determined to do it.

I went home, and the very next day when Daniel got home from work, I sat him down on the living room floor, and I absolutely destroyed him. At one point he asked me if this was just a cruel joke. I told him it was not. Secretly, I was hoping that he was going to tell me to leave and never come back. I didn't want to be the one to make the decision; I wanted him to be responsible for breaking up our relationship.

But the most remarkable thing happened. He told me he wanted to work it out. I actually told him that he couldn't do that. He said he wanted us to get counseling and try to make it work. We decided—against my will—to get counseling. We would go separately at first.

Looking back, I can tell you now that something very powerful happened when I told the truth, and I didn't do it because I was trying to please God. Admitting to what I was, to say it out loud, helped me take some sort of responsibility and ownership for it.

After my confession, we tried to live together but that lasted maybe four weeks. I still wanted to live my life my way. Dan was so broken;

he was living in a personal hell as he tried to deal with the disgusting information I had given him.

He cried desperately, but I couldn't feel an ounce of compassion for him. I was the one who had done this to him, and it didn't bother me at all. He couldn't deal with all the imagery in his head from all of the things that I had told him. He was in constant agony and tears. He had trouble working, couldn't eat, and couldn't sleep.

Eventually he moved out; he just couldn't stand to be in the same space with me. As far as I was concerned, my marriage was dead, and I didn't feel anything for him. Nothing. I didn't love him, and I didn't like him. I just didn't feel anything at all toward him.

When he left, I was relieved. Now I was living on my own, in my own space without the hassle of a broken and sad man in my way. I could do whatever I wanted to do. I decided not to go to Brazil. I was recently unemployed, so I had all the time in the world to work out at the gym and entertain myself.

During this time I had a strong compulsion to keep on being honest. As I met with the counselor, I just told the truth, and it actually felt good.

Daniel came back two weeks after he had left and told me that I was the one that would have to leave our home because I was the one who had made the decision to destroy our marriage. That threw me for a loop. He gave me a few days to get packed and figure out what I would do.

But he also did the kindest thing—he made arrangements for me. I could decide to accept them or not. He arranged for a couple from church to take me in while we were separated. He said it was the hardest thing he had ever done because he had no idea what my reaction would be or where I would go.

I had a huge dilemma. I called lover number two, and he told me this was the time. I should move in with him and be done with it. Something prevented me from taking him up on his invitation.

I decided to accept the offer to live with the couple from church. It was a Saturday night and Dan helped me move. He asked me if I would go to church in the morning and sit with him. I agreed to meet him there.

That night I was at the bottom. I realized how desperately messed up I was, that I was completely powerless to make permanent change for the good in my own life. I had nothing left. I was unemployed, out of my home, out of my comfort zone, no phone to contact people except the home phone. I didn't even really have anyone I could call. I had shut out pretty much everyone in my life. I felt hopeless. In my mind, I decided that I must surely be a person that God could not forgive. My head ached in a way I cannot describe. It was the worst night of my life.

Remarkably, God did not allow me to be in that state for very long. The next morning I went to church. The pastor preached a sermon about being created for relationships. It was directed at me. The Holy Spirit moved me, the Lord called my name, and for the first time in my life, I surrendered. I went to the church altar and wept. I wept for everything. I cried a river that day. I had no idea what would happen next, but I did know that I wanted to finally surrender to the call to live for Christ. It was different this time. I went to my host home that Sunday night, and I had hope and peace, priceless, unbelievable peace.

The next morning I was sitting at the kitchen table journaling my experience from the day before, and I happened to look up at the Bible open to the page where devotions had been done that morning. This verse was highlighted in larger print than the rest of the text:

"For God alone, oh, my soul, wait in silence. For my hope is from him. He only is my rock and my salvation, my fortress; I will not be shaken" (Psalm 62:5).

It was a word specifically for me for that moment. It was the first time this had happened in my new walk of faith, that God gave me a *rhema* word. It defined exactly how I felt—hopeful. It was the first time I had hoped in years. It felt wonderful to allow myself to truly feel something real again.

I spent the next three months living at this couple's home. I was unemployed, so I went to the gym every day, and I went for counseling once a week. I read the Word for hours on end. I prayed a lot. I started attending a Bible study for ladies.

I remember going to that first meeting. I decided it must be good for some, but this was probably not where I needed to be. The next week I called the hostess, intending to tell her that I wouldn't be there that night.

But as soon as she heard my voice she said, "Oh, hi Jennie! I'm so glad you called; I can't wait to see you tonight."

I was too wimpy to tell her that I was calling to cancel, so I went, and I finished the course. The truths taught in the ladies study group changed me. More accurately, the Word of God changed me. Through the teaching of biblical truth, and through the sometimes painstaking copying out of the Word of God, truth began to seep into my heart and my head. For the first time in my life, I was learning how to study my Bible for myself. I couldn't get enough of God and His Word. I was having prayers answered almost as fast as I could pray them. It was a powerful time, and I can see the clear hand of God in orchestrating the events of my life to draw me to Him.

Things between Dan and me did not get better during our time of separation. He struggled hard. He battled my past all alone. His mind was awash with the horrible things I had done. He also struggled with my newfound faith. He couldn't believe that I could just become intimately acquainted with Christ after the life I had led. He couldn't understand why he was struggling so badly with his walk with God and I was "on fire."

We went on a few dates, and they were very hard. He was rightfully angry, and it spilled out of him. He struggled with the decision to stay in the marriage at all. According to the Word of God, he had every right to walk away, and he went back and forth between deciding to just end our marriage and trying to rebuild it.

Something dramatic happened to my vision when I came to the Lord. I saw Dan as I remembered him. My feelings for him began to grow. Real, genuine love, a love that would give and build up, a love that was not self-seeking, a love that would sacrifice. I never lost hope. I believed that God would put us back together again, even though I didn't really have a reason to.

Dan was so angry and tormented it seemed a bit unreasonable to believe that he could ever love me again, but I was sure he would. I didn't know how long it would take, or what it would take to make it happen, but I trusted and allowed God to work on me in the separation.

After we had been separated three months, we met with a couple who encouraged us to live together again if, indeed, we were committed to making our marriage work. That same night Dan invited me to come home, and I accepted.

The first year was so hard for me. The temptation to go back to my sin was strong. It was what I had known for so many years and Satan surely did not want us to succeed. There were a few actions I was led to take to avoid the well-worn habits that would have quickly returned me to my life of sin.

I resolved to stop listening to any music that did not honor Christ. Music is so powerful for me, for the good and for the bad. I had to give up any and all music that caused my thoughts to return to a time or place that did not bring glory to God.

I resolved to stop watching any television that went against clear scriptural teaching, any show that condoned adultery, lies, killing, or any other God-mocking behavior.

I also gave up reading most books that I would have devoured in the past. I love a good story and I am an avid reader, but I simply cannot make room in my mind for things that do not clearly line up with scripture. My previous selection of magazines was the one other thing that I had to be done with.

The last and most important step I took was something that a Christian lady taught me. She said that if I asked, God would always provide the out. In any circumstance where I might be tempted, all I needed to do was acknowledge that I could not fight it on my own and ask God to please provide me a way. He did, every time. Either the phone would ring and distract me, or He put a song in my heart that encouraged me, or He brought scripture to mind that I had been busy memorizing. But always He provided the way of escape. With each success, I was strengthened to do the right thing more quickly the next time.

I know now that this is a promise God makes to me in scripture and it holds as true today as it did that first year out of my life of sin. Listen to this promise:

> No temptation has overtaken you but such as is common to man; and God is faithful, who will not allow you to be tempted beyond what you are able, but with the temptation will provide the way of escape also, so that you will be able to endure it.
> —1 Corinthians 10:13 NASB

I got through that first year without a return to the sin that had held me captive for so many years. Having been obedient so many times in a row, the struggle became less and less, and then I was tempted less frequently to return to that life. This verse in James explains my victory over my past:

> And prove yourselves doers of the word, and not merely hearers who delude themselves … But one who looks intently at the perfect law, the law of liberty, and abides in it, not having become a forgetful hearer, but an effectual doer, this man will be blessed in what he does.
> —James 1:22,25 NASB

Each act of obedience brought blessing. God has given me a desire to meet Him every day. It has been six glorious, hard years, living in relationship with Christ. I meet Him every day, even if it's just for a few moments. I love to read the Word. I am often surprised at changes He is bringing about in me. I am now sickened by my past. I wouldn't even tell my story if I didn't think that somehow it could help someone else.

But it can, because my story tells you there is hope. Sin can be overcome; lives can be restored; and Christ can make the ugliest past into a wonderful story of grace and mercy.

STUDY GUIDE

IF YOU WOULD like to turn this book, *Transforming Keys,* into your own study guide, you can do what every woman who has explored these "Keys" in depth has done while attending the course itself! The track is very simple, and the tools are easily handled.

- First choose your own notebook, personalize it, and decorate the front if you would like to.
- Pray and ask the Holy Spirit for His help.
- Now, as you read each chapter, on one side of the open page write out both the scriptures and the word definitions. You will soon find them to become meaningful and applicable.
- On the opposite side, the blank page, write down your own understanding, thoughts, and questions, and anything you believe God is saying to you.
- Periodically go back to both review and update the personal side.
- You will be amazed to find you are journaling your own journey towards the Lord, and that both your mind and heart have expanded in a wonderful way.
- The truths you embrace will begin to enhance your relationships powerfully and almost imperceptibly.

CPSIA information can be obtained
at www.ICGtesting.com
Printed in the USA
LVOW12s1137141117
556219LV00001B/2/P